CW01481352

MIRRORS

Alex Heaton

UPFRONT PUBLISHING
LEICESTERSHIRE

ISBN-1-84426-206-5

Published 2003 by
UPFRONT PUBLISHING
Leicestershire

Printed by Lightning Source

MIRRORS

Contents

Houses

The house Jack built
Is the house Jack died in.
Houses are homes
To be laughed and cried in.
Houses are holidays
And prisons for others
Of happy marriages
Or feuding lovers.
Houses witness girls and boys
Of carpets cluttered with books and toys.
Houses witness the single and old
Of sad Christmases
Where it's lonely and cold.
Houses are places
Where people persist
They are born into the world
Then cease to exist.

November Nights

November mist creeps
Along heartbroken streets,
Love lies torn asunder.
Frozen thoughts loom ahead
It's a million years since summer.

Out of a mountain
Appears a hand
Begging for that of another.
Words are drowned
By the wind all around
Screaming along with the thunder.

Planting flowers an idle dream
Of those caught in an age
Threads of life cut with a knife
Gripped like iron from our cage.

Houston, We Have a Problem

Something's wrong
It's too hot in here,
Goddamit! Houston, can't you hear?
Our pleas for rescue from this ship
Only one engine working,
I'm dizzy – can't seem to get any air
Who planned this mission to an empty nowhere?
To rocky, poisoned, lifeless worlds
Of a spaceship crypt.

Without any sun, wine or girls,
Don't think we're gonna make it
All the way back home.
We're on fire now
Fumes taking their toll,
We'll just burn into oblivion
Of extinction so far
An unattended funeral
Of a forgotten star.

Let the Kids Speak

Young and innocent
Fair and handsome
Holding an adult world to ransom
Withholding the secret
To a life of joy
Sole prerogative
Of a little girl and boy.

Telling the grown up world out there
That it's so selfish
And never seems to care
And that it should take a look
And a leaf out of a children's book.

Because little lassies and little lads
Know so much more than mums and dads
They are wiser when it comes to things
As how best to treat other human beings.

Old Couple

Ned and Nellie Robinson
Eighty years old the pair of them
Signing for a Post Office giro
Scratchy signature of a cheap old biro.

They've loved each other through and through
Always done what each wanted to do
Raised three kids who've long grown up
Moved away and who they don't see much.

Ned puffs his Woodbines,
Nellie brews the tea,
Sharing memories of what used to be;
Sunday walks along a forest path
The park, barbers shop and café.

They tenderly grasp each others hand
Think of their long years in this land
Upon one another they can always depend
Accepting things gracefully, staunch to the end.

Insecurity

Around market stalls
The rich get insured
Against being unhappy
And not being bored.
Concern is shown on lined grey faces
With raindrops running down
Fast attempts to buy a life
That doesn't wear a frown.
Limousine stands close by
Chauffeur behind the wheel
Wishing his boss every success
In trying to seal the deal.

A million quid for just one good friend
A billion for a loving wife
And all the resources he can possibly pull
For an ordinary, simple life.

Motorway

Same old thing
The daily drive
Down grey grooves
Of an ebbing life.
Speedometer says he's nearly sixty
As people wave goodbye
Battery check says he's really low
On a countdown waiting to die
Fuel gauge says he's running out of juice
And nearly over the hill
Being overtaken by fast new cars
Whilst he's braking and it's making him ill.

Great Rivers

Biographies begin
As suffocated springs
From a fusion of raindrops
A paternal storm brings,
Pressing against earthy mountain wombs
Or running blind in underground tombs.
They rush for the surface
In rash infant haste
In sparkling effervescence
Of subterranean taste.

Absorbing subtle colourations
Of greens and browns,
Then sent to hell to crawl through towns
Choking from toxic industrial dyes,
Poisoned beneath steely skies.

And yet!
Gliding through meadows
On lazy Sunday afternoons
With bluebottle buzz and kingfisher tunes,
Creeping between lovers' toes,
Green and graceful
As through Summer it flows.

But immortality is not possessed,
As looming coasts
Spell an end to the quest;
But as a prisoner of man
At last it is free,
Bowing out in a glory to a heavenly sea.

Cold

Dripping icicles
From warehouses black
Spider webs, creeping moss
Windows smashed and cracked.

January morning; sun so pale
Winter's grey anonymous veil,
Claws so cold ripping through
Remaining warmth inside of you.

Smoky sky, crawling cars
Exhaust fumes, frozen hours
Lonely robin feeling the cramp
Subdued citizens, long faced, damp.

Laughing Castles

Fingers point
At the funny little man
The odd one out
They took away in a van
The one who stares into space
Laughs all the time
And wears a simple smile on his face.
The one they say
Who was put away
Lives on top of a hill
In a fortress grey
Of ECT
Not like you or me.

But daily we shudder
In our rational homes
In winters of doubt and fear,
So perhaps those who live
On the hill
Are not as different
As we think they appear.

Girl in a Woman

She grew to be so tall
That once tiny child
Who walked the miles of infancy
And then the teenage trials.

She grew to be what always she
Had so very much desired
A woman who could choose to live
With more choice than a child.

Yet often she felt life gave neglect
Of the softer things gone missing
Such as the freshness of being still young
And her mothers maternal kissing.

Fat Cat

Rolex lies in the rain
Ticking in a gutter
He's been rushed into intensive care
His heart began to flutter,
Too much food
Too much wine
Too many cigars
And party time
Too many mansions
And limousines
Distant vacations
Investment schemes.

His fortunes he kept until the last
Held onto until he thought
The scare had passed
But he wasn't lucky
And now cobwebs lie
Upon the money
That let him die.

Invisible Men

Gone underground
But not down the pits
Just vanished men
Disappeared into mist.

Orgreave's funeral
Scargill's last stand
Pits shut down
Across the land.

All gone quiet now
Pitheads rust
Lungs still bleeding
From the dust.

Redundancy pay
Passes time away
Sitting at home
Lives fading away.

Little lad sees his dad's smashed face
Useless future of a grimace
Ripped up pride of unemployed shame
Hoping no one remembers his name.

Old Snaps

A human museum
Of recollection
Rushing the past
Into reflection
Seen from a misty eye
Wishing people didn't have to die.

The eye sees faces
In summer dress
Alert and fresh
With youth blessed
Feels no cobwebs
Nor smells stale air
Sees only an immediacy there.

Light is fading
Night draws in
Time to put the snaps away
Sleep tight with thoughts
Deep into the night
Of those not too far away.

The Spill

Got into the village water supply
Made the residents ill
The chemical company concerned
Denied any part in the spill.

Birds began falling from the skies
Leaves fell in spring from the trees
Much wildlife ceased to exist
Wiped out by the new disease.

There was a heated meeting in the Town Hall
The locals blamed those up top
Then the police came in to break it up
And the enquiry came to a stop.

Since then the firm has expanded
Assets stand at a billion dollars
Whilst babies are born without any eyes
And have to face tomorrow.

Closed Down Cafe

Lemonade serenade
Steaming summers
Ice cream dreams
Laughing lovers,
Blue sky of July
Trees of green
Winter unseen.
They came from hell
One we know so well
A season in for the kill
Made gales of a breeze
Brought summer to its knees
Froze faces with its chill.
Cafe doors creaked
Its hinges of rust
Inside a gloomy crypt of dust
Ghost town of a season gone
Winter's wrath rushing on.

Unfinished Drinks

Our toast
Of brimming glasses
Around us envious glances,
We danced, held one another tight
Loved deep in the heat of the night.
But then you told me of somebody else
Who touched your heart the most
I left the bar
Drove home alone in my car
Knowing in my tears you were lost.
The wine was sour
I'd got it wrong
It wasn't to happen,
It didn't belong
In what they call the real world
Where life often brings
In the sad shape of things
Love's flight of farewell wings.

The AIDS Carrier's Version of His Death

'I'm sorry,' I said
Arching up from the bed
Before collapsing in a heap of fatigue,
The nurse looked on – all part of the job
That death is simply routine.
What is this spectre, this disease
Hideously breaking me into bits?
Medication useless
Impatiently the great leveller sits.

I would if I could
Exchange all my bad blood
In some pure mountain spring,
A futile transfusion which is an illusion,
A mirage that mercy can't bring.

For the past six months
People have entered my room
All saying how sorry they feel,
Would it make it any better
If I never had loved,
Just a heart of celibate steel?

Offended whispers about me being gay
By people who don't understand what they say
Yet I wouldn't change the past by a single day
Because how I've lived has been my way.

I don't believe in God, I've never had the faith,
Just a love of other human beings,
But now it seems that was not enough,
Love's betrayal of a fatal wasting.

Sometimes at night there's a need to cry
Like heavy rain clouds in the sky,
Letting everything out, all the good, all the bad,
Drowning in tears of a future I cannot have.

All They Had at the Time

Only had what was available
Only did what they were capable
So criticism is often undeserved
Of former times from which we've learned.

Past practices may seem cruel
Harsh without compassion
But at the time it seemed quite fine
All part of their cultural fashion.

Always remember that we today
Who are civilised or so we say
Are often worse than times long past
And room for improvement will always last.

Dreams of Dust

Lying in a basement
Before I was born
Before my blood could run
I lived far beneath this world
Below this world's sun.

From deep in the basement
I heard shouts from above
Saw my father's face
Felt my mother's love.

That was long ago
And time has been cruel
I wander the house
A doddering old fool.

I crouch in the attic
And see yellowed snaps
Of faces whose time
Has long since passed.

Heart so sore, mind is worn
No trace of the place I was born
Wings heavy with mortal time
Tomorrow might not be a day that is mine.

Never Tell You

Never tell you do politicians
About motives behind their decisions
Or why they fail to answer a question
Turning the talk in another direction.

Never give you the real truth
Only propositions devoid of proof
Of why their policy is sure to succeed
Except for self enhancement and greed.

Secret summits behind closed doors
Denying they ever started wars
Branding the opposition as absurd
Schooled in lessons of empty words.

Crumbling Bridge

Meet me halfway
Same time, same place
Before the middle disappears
Or we'll lose the race.
Meet me memory of a past long gone
The same old road, you know the one,
Where we first met face to face
Meet me at the bridge
Before it's too late.

City of Slumber

Tired lights,
Drowsy cars
Rain on a pavement
A dying day yawns,
Lies down in smoke and smog deep
In urban slumber-land
In concrete sleep.

Tiny traffic now
Empty streets
The urban giant so long on its feet,
Metropolis mother
Turns out the light
Of a day like any other
And sinks into the night.

Life's Too Short

Met a girl on a freezing day
Warmed each other as we lay
Upon the snow, upon the ice
A one-off thing but it was nice.

Met an old lady in a grocers store
Said her landlord was demanding more
Money for the upkeep and bills
I thought poverty's a thing old as the hills.

Met a copper at a busy junction
With snowflakes upon his coat
He said he was off with the wife and kids
Next summer to Spain in a boat.

Met my Granddad in the local pub
Listened to his story as best I could
So noisy the jukebox and the chatter
He said I looked pasty and was getting fatter.

Met myself in the mirror that night
Had to look again, something wasn't right
I'd aged ten years in a single day
Listening to those with so much to say.

They're Coming to Take Me Away

They say they've finally got the man
The one who did the crime
They're coming in a big black van
I can hear the sirens whine.
I count down the moments
Till they break down the door
I know who it is they're looking for
It's me and very soon I'll no longer be free
I'll be down on the farm with the ECT
I suppose it had to happen this way
My destiny undertaken
And now they're coming to take me away
With thirty years forsaken.

Loving Life, Dreading Death.

Life is my dearest friend
Death my enemy who waits at the end
Life the flower and moving of limbs
Death the leveller who lays me still.

Life the sparkle in my eyes
Life the sound of things around
Death the rotting into ground.

Life the gift of a short lived second
Death the curse with which to be reckoned.

Across the Bay

Echoes of frozen seagulls shriek
Across cliffs
Above waters deep
Rainy skies
Seeds of the sea
Consummating it's destiny.
Fishermen rub calloused hands
Beginning another day
Nets are dragged across the sands
Shadows of dawn creep away.

Thundering

Steel sky
Cracked a thousand times
The fury
In ragged, jagged lines
A storm drowned
A million birds
In violent torrents of a swirl.
Thunder cannoned
From coast to coast
Ripped the ocean
Shattered boats
Smashed cities
And deafened the world.
The thundering everywhere was heard.

Weeks of Rain

Rain came
Rinsed away
Mud on our faces
Where we once played.
Now a shopping centre
Stands in that place
There is no mud
Only tears on my face.

Drowned as I became adult
Rush push living
In a tumult
Casino syndrome
Cash over care
Off to a future
Leading nowhere.

The rain was cool
But could only clean so much
And as I feared it disappeared
We got so out of touch.

Girl with the Green Shoes

With her long red hair
And flaming attire
It seemed she couldn't lose
As everybody stopped to stare
At the goddess
In the strange, green shoes.
Seduction her function
Knew no bounds
Not once did she sing the blues,
But it all came tumbling down
For the goddess
Of the strange, green shoes.
Greatest diamonds in the world
Shone from sultry skin
Nobody could afford to buy that girl,
But her luck was running thin.
Had everything any woman could wish
Could easily pick and choose,
But left love too late
And the world wouldn't wait
Lonely lady of the strange green shoes.

Always a Loser

Can't deduce means from ends
Loads of enemies
Zero friends,
Always raining, days so cold
His life a crying, dying world.
The future extant
The present destroyed
The past a memory of a void,
No job, home, kids or a lover
Has only himself
That and no other.

Race We Run

It's said along the grapevine
Of tried and tested time
That one day things
Will all turn out fine.

I'm told by those
Who are wise and know
That no matter what the pain
We all come in from the rain.

It's written that despite the tears
And no matter what the cost,
Stars will shine at the finishing line
For those who thought all was lost.

But I wonder sometimes
About this race
And the world in which it lies,
If for some there's no space
And never a place
Where peace and happiness lies.

Crystal Colours

Chink of glassware
Splits the light
Into rainbows
Of a long lost night,
Colours, shapes, visions and sounds
Coalesce into crystals
I have found.
A life I was given
To do and to be
Like the rainbow
Arched to infinity,
But it faded fast
Stole my time
I never used to think I would die.
Crystal colours are shades of grey
The rainbow is gone
Along with my days
New people walking
About in life,
Young crystals of colours bright.

Sex in Space

In our silver spacesuits
And self ventilating boots
We left earth behind
For something new to find.
Made love on the way
All night, all day
Unstopping sexual shopping.

I bought your love
In a cosmic currency
Past so many stars
Away from Earth's redundancy.

It all fell through
So long ago
A green world soured
With nothing left to show.

So we blaze new erotic paths
Dance upon dreams of a distant past
You touch me here, I touch you there
On route to a climax we both can share.

Rain on a River

My reflection stared at me
As I stood by the river
In the rain,
And another face
That wasn't there
With green eyes and blonde hair
Was by the side
Of loneliness I needed to hide.
From all directions
The rain assailed
Reflections starting to fade,
She still didn't come
And I knew never would
In the mirror of a river I'd made.

Too Late Now

Burning candles
A hundredfold
Of my time
Till I've grown old
Too late now to start again
The past is buried
It ended then.

You have changed
And so have I
Moved into different
Ways of life
Unable now to slot back in
To what is gone.
We can't right the wrong.

Forget what was
Let it go
Cry if it makes
It easier to do so.
But don't think
The past is the present now
Dreams are what life
Doesn't allow.

How Did I Know?

Half closed curtains,
Misty eyes
Gathering clouds of ragged skies.
Only fifty-six
But on his last legs
A disease whose outcome
Could only be death.
Didn't hear the doctor's whisperings
To his children and his wife
That very soon in a sad bedroom
He'd exit from this life.
So instead of a cure
Of which there was none
They gave him coloured water
As though nothing was wrong.
His grandson so young
Only just conceived
Asleep across the street
With tiny hands and feet
Oblivious to goings on
So everybody assumed
But were to be proved wrong
For at two o'clock exactly
When the poor man died
In a pram across the street
The baby cried.

Forgotten Songs

There's a mill by the stream Nellie Dean
My old man said follow the van
His master's voice no longer around
Gone too, the big band sound.

Gramophone, saxophone
Cobwebs in my mind
A cluttered life of getting old
Few melodies come to mind.

Piano keys, arthritic knees
Distant days of being young
In cold rain I shower today
A heartbeat a silent drum.

Mountains of Gold

There he lies on a four-poster bed
In his kingdom of gold
But it is cold and dead.
Made fortunes great
Built mountains high
Of brightest gold
Rising into the skies.
His mansion of a hundred rooms
Is shrouded in sepulchral gloom
The empty echoes have no host
Only that of a wealthy ghost.
So there he lies
Amidst gathering flies
Eyes fixed upon a wall
At grand masters of faces past
And now he joins them all.

Nobody Knows

Stigma upon the imbecile
Tears of a motherless child
Walking wounded of this life
But nobody knows why.

Lonely lady without any friends
Old man's time nearly at an end
Often you love even though you try
Yet nobody knows why.

Streets of futureless youths
Politicians who don't tell the truth
Fodder for factory and war machine
Caring society an idle dream.

Rainy days of pain and blood
Gathering of the misunderstood
Still searching after countless years
For the reason why which never appears.

Spaceman

Since a kid
He dreamed of far away worlds
Newly born stars, galactic swirls
Tried to comprehend space and time
But it proved too much
For his mortal mind.

Then when he died
It all opened up
And he flew past shining stars
Travelling at the speed of light
Amongst angels past Venus and Mars.

He got further
Than he ever thought he could
But stayed restless in his mind
For his only home was
The place he had left
Of planet Earth
So far behind.

Sparrows

Woman and man
Limited to a lifespan
Braving the weather
Two sparrows together.

Winter so cold
The screaming gale
So much lost
With gathering moss.

What gleams becomes dull
What shines turns to rust
What's new grows old
And all turns to dust.

Lost Morning

As kids we raced down dusty lanes
Bright faces in the rain
Over fields and over hills
Heading for the rainbows end.

It seemed a lifetime getting there
And that's exactly what it was
A journey with a common end
Undertaken by all of us.

That lost morning did exist
But in my mind it's buried in mist
Rainbow falling to the land
Awaiting every woman and man.

The Trunk

This dress once caught
Soldiers' eyes,
As did this necklace,
Bracelets, rings;
All now layered in mothballed dust,
A generation forgotten
No longer in touch.
Yet so alive these possessions
In an attic of peeling paint
Voices of their owners
Far off, faint,
Tear-jerking nostalgia
Eyes of sentiment bright
Like a much missed Ouija game
Tonight.
Faded photos yellow tinged
Curling at the ends
Faded faces of loved ones
Acquaintances, friends
Looking up with an immediacy
Of the instant now,
Unbounded by time as only love can allow.

Don't go to Sleep

In the haunted house
If you nod off
Something might creep up
Knock your head clean off,
Might tie you up, tear off your face
Give you such nightmares
You'll always stay awake.
This house is black
It reeks of evil
It's walls are stuffed
With murdered people.
Candlesticks drip
Molten wax and blood
Dead faces laugh
From ceilings above.
This house is hell
Even for a moment
It always has been
Full of torment.
Bats shriek
Dobermans bark
As daylight fades
Gives way to the dark.

Space Travel

So we took off
Cut links with Earth
Made a big break
Our greatest mistake,
Spent centuries searching
For bright new worlds
Found nothing except
Our own sad souls.

Went where nobody
Had gone before
Yet found no beginning
Only the exit door,
Wasted so much money
And so much time
Travelling to nowhere
With broken minds
And returned a lot later
To the world we'd disowned
Knowing deep in our hearts
We had to come home.

Gardens We Knew

Sleeping on the lake
Lilies we didn't wake
As we ran around fountains
In days of ice cream,
Now it all seems a dream.

Trees which bowed so low
Kissing the earth
Consummating any love
Left in the world,
Trying to give it new birth.

Childhood times of nursery rhymes
I heard them and I'm glad
I' d like to be young again if I could,
But youth is only once to be had.

Prayers in Hell

I repent
After where I've been sent
I'm sorry about my past
If you'll only give
Me another life
I'll be better behaved
Than the last.

It's hot in here
Giving me grief
This raging heat
I'm stuck in beneath.

Let me rise up
Higher than the stars
To where the more fortunate dwell
Heaven just has to be
Better than this
Infernal exile in hell.

Frost on a Field

Summer came
With loving rain
I ran by the river
Of a warm, bright day,
The sky trembled
Blushed deepest of blue
Summer was the only
Loving I knew.
Laughter filled my hours
Of a life full of flowers
Even scarecrows spoke
Of lives full of hope.

But one evening
Shadows never seen before
Crept across the land
With icy hands
And above and below
There began to fill
A flooding in
Of winter's chill.
Summer so old
Came to an end
And when summer died
I lost a good friend.

Cruel

Splintered wineglass
Grasped in wrath
Bloody fingers of
An argument's aftermath.
Wicked words said
To hurt and wound
Which only a long time
Can now soothe.
Vicious revelations
To surprise and shock
Cruel accusations
Meant to mock
One's humbleness
Which is not returned
Only meeting eyes
That continue to burn.

Walk through the Park

We see a tramp
In a trench coat damp
Coughing up blood
Like a crimson flood,
We hear a policeman
Shouting at a youth
Demanding an explanation
Which had better be the truth.
We see an old lady
Of shoes worn out
And a passing financier
Whose never gone without,
We hear a child crying unseen
That there's too much concrete
And too little green.
We see all these souls
Caught in the rain
Denied so much love;
Will things ever really change?

Oceans Ahead

They have overtaken us
Reached a further place than us
Closer to finishing the race than us
More remote in space than us.

They have surpassed us
Left us behind
Have got there before us
With new things to find.

They are the dead
Who are oceans ahead
Immune to ignorance
And this world's dread.

Staring up at the Stars

What's up there
Infinite night
Of blackness without any end,
Who is up there
Perhaps no one at all
Those stars are nobody's friend.

Is it all here? Perhaps,
And only here full stop
That anybody speaks,
Because above in empty spaces
Dwell only cold faces
Of stars that shine
Without love for thine.

Shopping for a Lost Soul

I stopped walking
And pulled out a wad
Of tenners and said
'Here you poor sod'
And the old man smiled
Then moved away
To buy his first meal
In over two days.
I saw a really nice Easter egg
Gave it to some kids
Who seemed to beg
For chocolate that was
Almost a dream,
Only crusts and scraps
Had most of them seen.
Gave a bottle of pop
To a thirsty young girl
Whose only pleasures were free
Who looked toward
What she couldn't afford
In the jungle of society.
Got back home
Stared at all my money
Realised lots of things
In life aren't funny
Still saw today's faces
Before my eyes,
Cried alongside this world's sad skies.

Under the World

Beneath our familiar
Carpets and streets
Is another world
We've yet to meet,
Further than foundation
Deeper than deep
A kingdom of
Wonderful endless sleep.

It's for souls grown tired
Of the rat race above
Pushy people
Who shout and shove,
It's always there waiting
Like a lifelong friend
Who welcomes you in
As you near this world's end.

Sad Child

Don't cry my child
Your life has barely begun
There are blue skies to live for
Cool air and sun
Trees and flowers
Your own laughter and smiles
As you travel down your life
Of a road many miles.

In your bedroom
Surmount the fear
No bogeyman is near
Only curtains which flap in the wind
And a blackbird outside
Who loves you and sings.

After the War

And so the settling
Of the dust
But only for those
Of the upper crust
Safe within walls
Of high command
Not rotting in fields
Under the ground.

Celebratory political toast
To a victorious host
No mention nor attention
Paid to those
Who now are only ghosts.

Sepulchral Avenue

Many times we walked
Ever so slowly
Ever so happy
Never felt lonely
Yet now I mop up my tears
Wings growing on remaining years.

Did I somehow sense
You wouldn't always stay
That your loving might move away
That there would be so little left to say
A chill in the wind those last sad days.

That long winter
When I rushed out to the shops
To buy you something
I feared you'd not got
Something like love
Which one day might be lost
Now I walk alone
Crippled by the cost.

Monument of Lost Meanings

Lived, fought and died
As these memorials testify,
Shot down from the skies
Or in flaming tanks fried,
Or lethal torpedoes
Giving watery death
Gasping for air
In inky depths.

Bullets that found
So youngest of hearts
Now just names
Carved in stone in parks.
And the rain falls
As it has for decades
Upon silent monuments
As children play
Laughing beneath freedom's skies
Thanks to those now only ghosts
Who gave up their lives.

Whirlpool

Dizzy feeling of drowning
Serious mood of frowning
Vortex of water whirling around
Sucking us in, dragging us down.
Centrepiece of fear
Waters drawing near
Claw snatching out
No one hears us shout.
Recurrent nightmare
Subconscious dread
Subterranean spells
Within our heads,
Billions of gallons
Down our throats
Smashing all lifelines
Breaking our boats.

Uncle Reaper

Uncle Reaper all in black
Face cracked of a ripe old age
He's been around since time began
In the wings of this world's stage.

Waiting and waiting
Always there
To slip in and take away
Those who've run
This life's hard race
Having reached the end of their days.

Circling around
Closing in
Swooping down
Claws dug in
Taking away
To a distant land
Those he clutches
In his time-worn hands.

Backdate

Inside his mind
Is an attic of a kind
A private museum
Priceless coliseum,
A temple where all
He's loved and known
Worshipping all the seeds he's sown.

Her attic is similar
Except it's downstairs
In a place called her heart
Of things important from the start.
So they forage for things
In lives gone by
Putting flesh on bones
Amass this, retrieve that
And their memories build new homes.

Gardens of Summers Gone

Will they ever return
Those bright early mornings
Mellow evenings
Soft shadows of ourselves?
Are we stuck in a grip
Of grey bitter winter
Of only sleep we ever know.
Ripe orchards
Lush fields
Green caress, fresh,
Birds tender feathers;
Come back those summers
And stop my tears
Because I can't stop crying
When I think of those years.

Who Will Help Them?

Child with ice cream
On it's face
Child with blood on it's face
Child who believed in Santa Claus
Child now with no faith at all.

Child who ran through
Fields of green
Kicked a ball in a school soccer team
Smelled salt of clear seas,
But walls of a prison
Is now all he sees.

Wakes up to vacuums, voids, spaces,
Fills in the gaps sniffing glue
Cannot laugh
There are no funny faces
And so little worthwhile to do.

A Common Road

Collective purpose
Communal endeavour
Team work, spirit
Or whatever,
Supposed unity towards a cause
As if it were a natural law.

Yet those endowed
With uncloned hearts
May well prefer
To remain apart,
Away from jungles
Of conformist sweat
Dying like robots
With lives to regret.

Mother Machine

Pear drop lobes
Of wise skin
Aged but still so young within
Pear drop lobes
Which wobble in the wind
Could accommodate earrings
A million fold.

So she sits there
Thinking through time
Always about
A different life,
But those tears
That run down her face
Are gladdest oceans
Of a wonderful place.

She's done so much
So much has she seen
Maternal watcher
Mother machine
Who knows far more
Than most could tell
Pear drop lobes
Of the sweetest of spells.

The Grey

Any ordinary, typical day
Of those at work
And those that play,
Passing cars, high street stores
Business as usual
The day opens it's doors.

Yet far away
Are the unseen grey
Behind lock and key
Of a different society
Of torn jackets and jeans
Sadness and screams
Electric shocks
All hope lost.

Pretty gardens and trees
Lend such hell a breeze
Of false innocence
Dishonest pretence.

What passes in the daily news
Of the sadly afflicted, poorly few
Is a time bomb which won't go away,
Will catch up with us all one day.

Silver Mermaid

She slides so gracefully
Swims effortlessly
Smiles lovingly
Of silver skin is she.

Deep, widest waters
Hold her with esteem
Respect from all sea creatures
She is lonely Neptune's dream.

Ancient yet so young
Many races run
Many faces charmed
Greeted with her arms.

She will always remain
Always stay
Deep down in oceans
All her days
Where it is quiet
Where there is peace
In love with wonders of the seas.

Lid on Your Love

Can't contain
Welling emotions
Bottled up love inside
Can't suppress deep devotions
Your heart you cannot hide.
Maybe most of us feel the same
When we see one whom we love
We feel we can never have enough.

Manhattan Man

Cool silhouette
She cannot forget
Leaning on a building
Calm, quiet
On a late September evening.
They met in a grocery store
In him great charm she saw
They had a meal, drank some wine,
Suddenly he vanished from her life.

She cries sometimes
Wonders where he went
Why he left her alone,
Did she do or say
The wrong sort of thing
Tall dark stranger
Please come home.

Santa's Grotto

He bounces a little boy
Upon his knee
It's a time of year
Called nativity,
He smiles at a girl
Who is shy
With a gleam of excitement
In her eyes.
The children's parents
Also smile
They used to see Santa too
But it's been a long while
Since they were bounced
Upon his knee
And childhood was
A time so free.

Somebody Out There (Is Looking for You)

Tap, tap on a window
Shadow on a wall
Can you sleep tonight
Or will your composure fall?
Believe it or not
Someone's after you
To pay back a disservice
You once put them through,
They can't forget
Cannot forgive
Nor cease to be angry
So long as you live.

Shopping (Can Seriously Damage Your Wealth)

Wallets, sporrans, purses
Piggy banks, savings certificates
Postal orders, IOUs,
All the shops want
Is money from you.
They will put up posters
That shine and sparkle
Allure you'to purchase
Within malls of marble
Of yucca plants
Neat, tidy fountains,
And security guards
As tall as mountains.
What's on offer is pretty and nice
Yet all such things have attached a price
But smiles will remain
Whilst ever you have money
But transform into frowns
Which are not so funny.
If you're poor
It's the exit door
Kicked out into the road
But if you're rich
It's a free coffee and sandwich
Indoors and out of the cold.

Lament for an Age

Broke their backs
Had houses like shacks
Lost limbs, sweated oceans
And died;
Victorianism
An industrial prison
Lost children and widows who cried.

Foul black air
Human wear and tear
Denied a share
Nobody to care.

Forgotten now
Slaves of an age
Stuck in unstopping cage
Some fell down
Along the way
Those who didn't
Did at a later day.

Dry history books
So few we now read
Of those forced to choke
On soot and smoke
Who never saw a flower now a field.

Dreading the Next Day

Soaked pillows of terrified sweat
Worse to come
But not quite yet
But will come early shafts of dawn
When tomorrow is so
Unwantedly born.

If only a day
Was a human thing
Then it would be great
To abort such a being
End it's life before coming out
Not announce itself
With an ominous shout.

Such is this young soldier's vigil
Before tomorrow
A massacre he knows,
One that will include himself
As minutes bring him
Closer to death.

Up the Drive

Up the drive
She's still alive
After all she's been through
The pain dished out
Along the way.
Carrier bag
Of fruit, cigarettes
Visiting her son
She fiercely protects,
He's been locked away
For thirty years
Her love undiminished
Her face without fear.

She knows quite well
In the back of her mind
That her son might always be confined,
Locked up till his dying day
But that's something
He never hears her say.
Instead it's chin up, keep smiling
As into the visiting hall she now is filing
Tears of hard years, stoicism burning
So long as ever this world keeps turning.

Dead Languages

They only talk
If you'll believe
That though they speak
They cannot breathe,
They will only see
You as a friend
If you subscribe to a life
After the end.
They have no truck
For those of us
Who talk of trivia
And make a fuss,
You'll only become
One of them
If you see a far future
For all women and men.
To see history as a factory
Of chaos and lies
Confusion and bloodshed
Of so many good lives
And you'll only know
Such things for sure
When you step through the very last door.

Where Are You Now?

Used to know you very well
But that's twenty years ago
Where did you go
Why did you leave me
What was it I did wrong?

Did I finally wear your patience
Take up and waste your time?
I'm truly sorry if I did
I'd like to apologise.

Often I make such stupid errors
I'm a fool too because I think it's clever
And people around me drift away
Vanish and I never see them again.

Please return, forgive me
I'm sorry for my stupidity
Another chance is all I wish
It's hell being all so lonely as this.

Bubblegum Fun

Street corner
Two boys, two girls
Blowing bubbles
In a teenage world,
Not old enough to go into pubs
So far able to stay off drugs.
They blow bubbles
Like massive balloons
Crack jokes about sex
Beneath a grinning moon,
Can't afford cars
Or to eat at The Ritz
But can buy ten fags
And a bag of chips.

Common Good

Some people try unselfishly
To add to the common good
It's a trait that should be a universal one
Oh! If only it could.
The little bit of help
To the old man
Assistance given to kids
Living in back street digs.
There's plenty of money in this world
But it has never been shared
That's because it's a greedy grasping place
Where only a few have cared.

Winter

Too remote to contemplate
Stranded snowman on a winterscape
Too sad when the sun doesn't burn
Cold crossroads wherever in vain you turn.

Futility of an icy cemetery
Rail tracks on your skin
Nailed down to nothing but zero
Neither out nor in.

Skies who hate and never love
Clouded caustic stare
Vultures wheeling horribly high
World without life laid bare.

Sand Lands

Dried up dreams
Of what once it had been
Rivers of life
Shades of green.

Metamorphosis
To cinderland
So perished life
Forever damned.

Atomic devils
Nuclear spells
Witchcraft turning
It all to hell,
Chipped, flaked
Crumbled, cracked
Desert days
No going back.

Lonely Lately

Have you walked alone
For so painfully long
You feel you're the only one?
A solitary sparrow
Stuck on a fence
Lonely, frozen and numb.
Have you looked out of windows
A thousand times
At all those people below
Whilst you did this
And then you did that
And nothing seemed to show?

But maybe those people
You see from your window
Are looking in at you
Feeling the same
Sad and lost in the rain
Every bit as broken and blue.

Suddenly I Cried

When I knew
I'd no longer see you
And all my flowers had died
I stood in the garden
On a winter's night
Looked up at the stars and cried.

It had been on the cards
That the glue of our hearts
Was breaking apart and decaying
And heaven above
Of cold stars without love
Didn't listen whilst I was praying.

Friends

A lonely life
Is a horrible life
A pretty useless time
So if you can
Always try and have some friends
Then the days will be more fine.

Being alone is like an empty home
No heating, sound or light
Just a dark, cold room
Of uneventful gloom
A life that just ain't right.

Never Be a Snob

It's a bad thing
To rabbit on
Boasting about oneself
Looking down on others
As inferior, worse or scum.
Everyone is not equal in life
As regards money, fortune and health
But all are equally deserving
To have a place
Upon this world's shelf.

Snobbery is a nasty disease
An unsightly blemish upon the skin
It makes people angry, hurt and sad
In a difficult world we live in.

When Somebody You Love Dies

If just the other day
One you loved passed away
It's a time of tears to flow
But if you're strong
Some pain might go.

Of course the pain
Will never fully go away
In wistful hours
It will cruelly stay
But try if you can
To keep soldiering on
Keeping busy, helping others
As strange life goes on.

Enjoy All the Seasons

If it's summer
Then of course
It's good to get out
See the brightness
Feel the breeze,
But if it's autumn
That's also good
Leaves diving from trees
In a wizened rush.
Then there's spring
Of new, fresh life
Soft green buds, baby lambs
Singing birds
Infant nature to love,
And even if wintertime is cold
Still give such a season a chance
Meandering footprints on snowy fields
Of lovers, eyes bright in romance.

They Never Did

Promised it all
Everything;
Delivered us only
Undeveloped film,
Reels of negatives
To buy the peace
Stalling long enough
Till our demands ceased.

Then another promise
Of a great golden age
To all work together for
On society's stage,
But the pledge was hollow
Our hopes run aground,
Promises, promises,
Empty sounds.

Numbers

Bricks in a wall
Is what it's all about
Nobody has names
Only robots to count
List, grade, select, assess
Aliens all of the same address.

Anonymous currents
Of amorphous beings
Drift in the breeze
Never heard nor seen
Silently screaming
For recognition
To others
In exactly the same position.

Death of a Dangerous Idiot

He worked on the pig farm
Wading in the muck
Of a melancholy mad world
In which he'd come unstuck;
At night he would lie awake
In the dark
Dreading tomorrow
When like the bite of a shark
They would pass a current
Through his head
Holding him down
On a cold steel bed.
Time after time visits
To the medicine cupboard
To see a white coated version
Of Old Mother Hubbard
Then back once more
To that electrical box
More fear, convulsions
Agony shocks.

Buttering his bread
With the same plastic knife
Undeservedly wounded
In a confused inner life
Simply left to fade away
Within walls of neglect
Till his dying day,
His worries ignored
His problems unsolved;
Scapegoating his madness
Was merely social control.

Deserts of the Heart

A flickering street lamp
Lights up love for sale
Flitting in furtive footsteps
Through someone's back door.

Most cities like ant colonies
Come alive at night
A language of glances
Fat wallets and back pockets;
Cars creeping through side streets
A pass, a signal, a come on; move.

The danger is concealed within clients' minds
The edge of a razor may be easy to find,
Drifting through the fearful winds of the night
Like a thousand times before hoping tonight's all right.

Melancholia

How we lived
How we loved
Yet only for so short a while.
Cancer came, thunderbolt of fate
Piling slush upon your smile.

And quite often these days
As I cry in my car
I wonder what and where you now are,
Maybe just dust
Mere thoughts in my head,
Once lovely and living
Now cold, gone and dead.

May

Warm but not
Excessively hot
Not humid
Not much rain,
The sort of month
You've been out for a walk
And want to go out again.

Baby lambs unsteady on their feet
Curious cows twitching their ears
The first wasp, first bumble bee
As a long summer vision appears.

Paranoia

He's looking at me
And so is she
It's all one big conspiracy
To prove me wrong
To put me down
I'm the only sane one walking around.

Spying on me through jealousy
They envy my superiority
Surveillance backed with ECT
Are they so daft as to think they've fooled me?

I shall win
I shall soar
Above all those
Who want to find our more
I shall triumph in my quest
Last one standing above the rest.

Rooms

Conversational drift
Sifting from mouths
Generations I long ago knew
The voices seem real
Or so they feel
Am I one of a fortunate few?

How can I tell
I know those words so well
Coming from faces
Of nostalgic places,
Reminiscence or futile thinking
Of a tired mind
And too much drinking?

As I sit
In a darkening evening
The rooms alive with heat
Of those I want to meet
Those to see eye to eye
Those who cannot die.

Mechanical

Sterile
Puritanical
Predictable
Mechanical
Oiled
Gleaming
No romance
No loving,
Only function
Alert to work
No satisfaction.
Task in a flask of a canister
A cold cask,
Feelings doused
Of steel
Barren,
Devoid,
Back to bed
In the cold garage
Human car
Motorcycle,
Machine so mean
Diabolical.

Far Away

Far away the land
I long to be
So we can be together
Like we used to be,
It seems so long
Since I saw your smile
Heard your voice
Muted now by the miles.

Moon may shine clear and bright
But is cold and empty
With no place in my life
But somewhere in space
Where you far away dwell
Is our much missed loving
I know so well.

The void is vast
The chasm between
What is and what is only a dream
Maybe some day I'll find myself there
Deep in space with your face
Of loving to share.

Maze

Entrapment
Within laborious situations
Soundless lives
Dead conversations.

Screwed up plans
Time ticking away
Ambitions thwarted
With each passing day.

Shattered pictures
Of non recognition
Jigsaw puzzles
With pieces missing.

And all the time
It's on your mind
That you're still looking
For what you can't find.

Sewage Street

Overflowing impurity
Rivers of toxic society,
Underground currents
Have no limit
Of poisons undiminished.

Sewage Street
Lapping your feet
Corroding your toes
Attacking your nose.

Buildings all around us crumble
Sinking into putrid rubble
Infecting our thoughts
Turning good blood to pus
We yield as Sewage Street
Conquers us.

Proximity Vicinity

Too close for comfort
Access denied
Keep out, don't trespass
Or you'll die.

Top secret
Stay well clear
Electrified fences
Don't come too near.

Official personnel
Screened and scanned
Classified data
From strategic command.

In the middle of nowhere
But crucial to the nation
Is all that's revealed
In state legislation.

Security cameras,
Dogs, guns,
Ready to turn your body to crumbs,
So keep out and stay out
Forget all you know
If you like your life
Want to see tomorrow.

Eternity's Too Short

To and fro
Back and forth
Throughout forever
Too familiar
Same old stuff
The universe isn't big enough.

Need more space
To see far more
Remotest stars
And planets born
Different life forms
Of alien kind
Eternity's far too short a time.

Is It All Lost

So far to come
Just to fall so fast
To stumble on a future
We thought would last.

We thought human jungles
Were of the past
But that now seems wrong
It's more dangerous
Than ever before
This jungle is lethally vast.

Kingdom without a King

Lonely hills
Barren clouds
For millions of years
They've counted the hours
Lifeless things
That do have a life
Even if mute
Cold as ice.

Deserts under dispassionate sun
Unloved rivers who for so long have run
Full of tears
Towards the sea
In a kingdom
Whose king will never be.

There Must Be Somebody

Bureaucracy means
It's hard to pin down
People you need to see
It's called red tape
A formal thing
Of a complex society.
Often you'll spend all day
Trailing round about town
Trying to see the person you want
But keep on getting put down.
Sign this form
Quote this number
Write to this address,
What's supposed to be fast and direct
Is a hell of a longwinded mess.

No Comment

Not one word of comment
Will you get from me
You're a nosey journalist
I don't want to see,
Don't wish to explain to
Nor elaborate
Go away I say
No comment.
Peering around
Peeping in
Inquisitively silly grin
Hoping to get from me a story
But you'll get nothing
To enhance your glory.

Bereavements

Gaping chasm
Of a loved one gone
Will make you cry an ocean
Sing sad songs
But you must try to keep on top
If you don't you'll fade away full stop.

Try to put other people in your life
They'll never substitute
But it adds a little light.
Keep busy, accept it's not unique to you
But a thing that everyone
Sometime goes through.

Invitation

Hello, come in, sit down, relax
Have a drink, help yourself to snacks
We've wanted to meet you for such a long time
Now we're glad that you've arrived.

It's party time all through the night
Tell us what sort of books you write
It must be expressive putting pen to paper
Any chance of a signed copy later?

Let me introduce you to everyone
They're keen to meet the literary one
Whose got best sellers in the States
Is modest and always understates.

You look tired, maybe a strong drink
Such as scotch and soda will help you think
And another sandwich won't go amiss
Oh, how we've looked forward to all of this.

Never on Time

You say you're my friend
But once again you're late
Why do you always treat me this way
Getting me in an angry state?

You promise to meet me
But break your pledge
Leave me high and dry
Hanging on the edge.

Then comes the excuse
That it won't happen again
And when it does you say sorry
That we still should stay friends.

But it's not funny, not a game
Because I bet if I treated you the same
You'd leave me without any hesitation
Which says very little for your consideration.

Vietcong Song

We weren't so stupid
Not so daft
To be unprepared for bomber aircraft,
So we built tunnels in advance
And all the bombs fell on lifeless space.

The ground peppered by B52s
Was a waste of explosive
That might as well not have been used,
All it did was make craters
Whilst we listened to the bangs
Laughing at Nixon and his Uncle Sam.

Nuclear

Mushroom forest
Of bleeding trees
Glow radioactively red
Roasted squirrel
Charcoal birds
Villages cremated, all dead.

Cities of silence
Melted cars
Whispers of the nuclear wind
Sighing in between
Buildings that flake
Bits of shrivelled up paint.

A telephone rings
A survivor wants to talk
But nobody picks up the phone
Most were all fried
And of those that didn't die
The caller is probably
No one you know.

Away from Here

Let's get out
Leave this behind
Move on, make tracks
In another life
Leave a doomed world
To it's grave
Transcend time
Unlock our chains.
Slaves of a planet
Of unhearing masters
History a catalogue
Of dread and disasters,
And now at last
We can leave it all
The prison-like lives
And break free from the walls.

Waited Too Long

I couldn't help waiting you know
I just couldn't stay
Felt I had to go.
That street corner
Where I waited for years
And you never turned up
Confirming my fears.

Someone else
Someone you saw
Different to me
In what way I don't know
But maybe one you thought
Was more worthwhile
Which makes me cry
Whenever you smile.

Disciples of the Dream

Followers of a shooting star
Which crosses the heavens
Of where we now are
Promises rewards
When our time is passed
Something enduring
Which will always last.

Bright comet
Lighting up the void
New life
After what was destroyed
Instilling all the sun in us
Awakening hearts of love.

Foreign Holidays

Splashing on lotions
Plastering on creams
Trying to get the deepest
Tan of your dreams
So as to tell the neighbours
Once back in town
About the hot sunshine
That nearly turned you dark brown.

About how much it cost
For a bottle of Coke
An ice cream
Or the naughty joke
The waiter cracked
On the last day
And how full was the lounge ashtray.
The size of the spiders
How hot it was at night
The beautiful bread
Toasted so light
The evenings of joy
With your passenger friends
And how you succumbed
To starting smoking again.

Beautiful

Her hair catches
All the lights
Her eyes moist
Her smile light,
Never treats people
On a first appearance
Not judgmental
Never fierce.
She's known so many people
She is wise and of course
So beautiful;
Everybody for miles around
When seen in her company
Feels warm and proud.

Redundancy

Despair,
Roads to nowhere
Miles and miles
Of smashed up smiles
Piled up memories
Of collisions
Where brakes didn't work
Due to no decisions.
Skies of fiery ruin
Hills of broken teeth
Only the sound
Of broken dreams underneath.

Distributional Virus

Computer zoomasters
Ready for it all
To take control once and for all,
Circuits logged
Into all we do
Why and when
And they are not our friends.

Built to assist us
In our lives
But they couldn't
Just stop at that,
They had to take total command
Loot our brains
And tie our hands.

Not Cut and Dried

Doesn't pay
Arrogantly to say
Everything goes to plan
That night follows day
That day follows night
That thing's will always stay.
One swallow doesn't make a summer
Such a bird won't always fly
Tomorrow is not the same as today
The only certainty is to one day die.

Have Fun

I know it's hard
To force a smile
When you're made to look
Such an imbecile
At an occasion
Such as this
A mess of guests
In loudest of jest.

I suggest we find
A quiet corner somewhere
Go for a walk
Get some fresh air
Because I too
Am feeling like you
Standing here so stupid
With nothing to do.

Bringing Out the Worst in Me

Ice on a river
Makes me shiver
I'll be rotten one day
Under the clay,
A skeleton
Of a life left behind
Dry dusty bones
Without a mind.

But right now
That's not the case
I'm alive and alert
Feeling great,
It's only the fear of my mortality
Which brings out the worst
Makes me unhappy.

Leaving Shadows Behind

There comes a time
When you have to make
A determined, clean break
With something that's been going on
You've never liked all along
It could be smoking
Drugs or drink
And you know that it's time
To seriously think
About cutting it out
Drawing the line
Because now you no longer
Want it part of your life.

Nobody Knows Nobody Cares

If an accident occurs
Out in the street
A call for help –
Someone else can sort it out.

Not me, oh! No!
I won't get involved
I've too much to lose
I'll leave it to somebody else.
Forty faces see the girl
Assaulted by the man
Yet not one of those forty venture out
To assist or sort it out.
Nobody cares
It's too much trouble
Busy world, violent ways
Just stay at home
Forget how to say hello
Save yourself, nothing more.

Soft Centres

Nearly bust a tooth today
Took lots of enamel away
Thought it was love
But it turned out to be steel
Like biting on a steering wheel.

So next time you're unfaithful
I'll be better prepared
Once bitten twice shy
Not sad or scared
I'll chew up the
Very heart of you
Not bite off more
Than I can chew.

Uncensored

Don't know how
It got smuggled out
From offices
Of censorship house
Rude, crude, utterly blue
A video starring me and you.

Filmed in Amsterdam
In a house owned by Madame
Shipped to the British Isles
Leaving us with embarrassed smiles.

What shall we do, throw it away?
If we're sussed we might be put away
For something surprising even to us
It's amazing what lust and money does.

Easy Way Out

Even a child
Could have guessed
That you were
Somehow possessed,
666 tattooed upon your spine
Thirteen of everything
In your mind.

You've ruined lots and lots
Of lives
Taking them by satanic surprise
But luck ran out
We got wise
Saw you for real
Behind your disguise.

We cast you out
Devil that you are
Exorcised you so very far
No longer to harm
The human race
Exiled to a very different place.

Oceans of Wine

Fountains of wars
Reddest of waterfalls
Cascading crimson below
Of lives that didn't see tomorrow.
All the grief, tears and waste
Such wine has the sourest taste
So very common, never rare
Through all history
Has been shared.

Lonely

I'm afraid that's me
But I wish it wouldn't be
I've so badly wanted friends
But I've lost all those
I thought I had,
All unhappy ends.

Do you ever feel
You're too much alone
And a need inside
For a friend?
A smile, a hug, embrace of love
To warm your frozen mind.

Spiders

So many people
Are scared stiff of you
Crawling upon their skin
It's a thing called a phobia
In case you didn't know
Who origins lie deep within.

It might be because
You've got so many legs
Or the way you crawl around
Or stay transfixed on a bedroom wall
Then suddenly drop to the ground.

Yet despite you instilling
Within people such fears
You are all excellent engineers
Architects of an arachnid kind
Spinning webs of beauty
From plans in your mind.

Mind Readers

Alien invasion
Data bleeders
Tuning in
To thoughts that feed us,
Innermost core of our minds
Essential essence
They will find.
Implanting a silicon chip so small
Behind your ear
You can't see at all,
Yet what it does
Is very nasty indeed
Draining thoughts
Upon which we feed.

Nostalgia

Textile mill
By the old canal
Sombre swans soaked in oil
Factories shut down
For quite a while
Tearful town, sad smile.

No more maypoles
No dog track posters
No blackberry picking
Only roller coasters
No public park
Of swings and prams
Just mobile phones
And traffic jams.
No room for kids to kick a ball
No slow conversation
No time at all
No clean river
No Morris men,
How I hate it now
How I loved it then.

Shown Up

Never before was I so embarrassed
Humiliated with shame
I never again wish to be seen with you
You don't exist. I don't know your name.

It's finally through
I never knew you
Since that horrendous day
When you ransacked my pride
And inside I died
Stuck for words to say.

How could you do it
Say such things
About me you supposedly loved?
I'll tell you something –
I'm moving far away
I'm sick of you
Had enough.

Misty Morning Chicago

Smokestacks criss-cross
Stressful skies
Still supporting the dream
Slaughterhouse rack
Of dripping fat
On route to a downtown canteen.
Plains of ever rising heat
The railroad never ends
Hedgehogs chewed up by harvesters
Where the poisoned Mississippi bends.
Curtains stay closed –
Six o'clock
Yellow cab squeals to a stop
Coffee vapour creeps
Up nostrils deep
Factories of oil asleep.
But the battery hen
Can't stop
Laying eggs for human greed
Cholesterolized mayhem
Shattered shield
Dead past, a forgotten field.

November

Dragging me down
Through swamp-like leaves
Mushy suffocation
Unable to breathe,
Shrouds of surrounding trees
Ghosts of November, mystery.

Unspeaking waters
Of a sullenness
Miserable dialogue between us
Antisocial lapping of waters drab green
To be frozen in winter
Their fate then sealed.

Train coughing through a valley
Windows opaque
From condensation,
A screeching brake
Approaching a station
Damp figures feeling old
Tired players on a platform
Of a drama so cold.

Parties

Have another glass of wine,
Sure man, I'm feeling fine
Feeling better than ever
I hear you're a writer
You must be clever.

This dress cost nine hundred pounds
The diamonds at least ten grand
And have you noticed the sapphire ring
Glittering on my hand?

Have another cigar,
On your vacation did you go far?
Did you meet lots of famous stars
Travel fast in luxurious cars?

Shall we go outside
For some fresh air
Or would you rather stay in?
It's a shame to waste
Such a wonderful night,
To be sensible would be a sin.

Meditation Through the Storm

You imagine
You live inside a cloud
In the middle of a terrible storm
You've always wished you were there
Ever since you were born.
Now at last you have that chance
To drink such heavenly rain
Fall back down into the sea
Only to rise again.

It's easy really
So simple to do
I've done it so often
So why not you?
Make the effort
Give it a try
Don't be ashamed
If you want to cry.

Sunflower

Summer was a dangerous game
Your scented seduction
Nearly drove me insane
Your sultry petals
Conspired with the heat
To make me dizzy
Sway on my feet.

You nearly got me you floral queen
Of yellow, red, violet and green
So nearly trapped me in your spell
Into your clutches I almost fell.

You were just a lover
Like any other
One hot, sticky July day
But phwoar! Did you turn me on!
The way your petals did play.

Pin Stripe Suicide

How long have we
Been prisoners here
In shelters of
Politically manufactured fear
Awaiting yet another
Whitehall instruction
Ending in poverty
Pain and destruction.
Industrial holocaust, shotguns of greed
Never giving people what they really need,
Lethal injection, electric chair
Drowning in our blood, dreaming of air.
Terminal undertaking, epilogue in the making
Everyone colliding, falling down dying.
Our bridges burning
There is no returning
Hysterical wailing
Sirens of our failing.
Mistakes a millionfold
Carved in stone
Of our temple of illusions
We could never disown.

Neptune

Neptune is the god of the sea
Has always been where he's wanted to be
Has always done what he could understand
Has always loved his watery land.

So far beneath this world's pain
In deepest depths of subterranean rain
And there he's been since the dawn of time
Living the coolest and peaceful of lives.

Over the Phone

A business deal
Of a million dollars
Negotiated down the wires
Or a mid morning natter
About the best fish batter
Between two bored housewives.

The obscene caller
With a husky tone
Breathing frustrations down the phone
Says he's watching your every move
Is calling from a nearby booth.

The kid whose got his exam results
Is top of the class in maths
Dials his dad, tells him the news
As his jealous sister laughs.

Or the private call between doctor and client
About a possible vasectomy
A number is discreetly disclosed
Which is of course ex-directory.

Local calls or international ones
All under this busy world's sun
People talking, sharing news
Gossip and points of view.

Saturn

Of all this planet's
Most beautiful things
Greatest of all
Are its shimmering rings
Of dusty glitter
Glorious sheen
Orange and golden
A cosmic queen.

Paint the World

Give sad canvas
A different face
From an obscene globe
Of a failed race,
A picture so different from old
Where paint is peace and truth is told.

Don't use black paint
That's like death
Don't use red paint
Of the devil's breath
Don't use yellow
It's a cowards skin
Just paint it all white
Without brushstrokes dim.

Make the seas green again
Make skies blue
With as much hope and sunshine
As you can possibly do.

Novemberscope

Roaring through the blackness
Warriors so cold
Soldiers of melancholia
Killers of summers old.

This is the take over
Invasion of ice
Fog and smog
Acid skies.

This is the creeping into cracks
Of winter's army clad in black,
The silencing of hopeful tunes
Funeral drums through the gloom.

Ice cream an ancient dream
Sunshine a dead friend of mine
Children's eyes no longer gleam
Summer something that used to be.

Churchyard Blackbird

She sings above cracked slabs
Crustiness of lichen
Moss encroaching
Weeds choking
Names long carved in stone.

Her songs of lament
For souls in the soil
Voices mute and stifled
Faces vanished from this world
No longer bright or smiling.
She sings so early
She sings so late
Until the sun sets
Once again on those whose fate
Was to remove a burden
As time grew old
Worn down and out
So still and cold.

The Only One

Lies and lies of radiography
Plus placebo chemotherapy
Massive medical insincerity
Death knell of its credibility.

So I prayed.

Six months left to exist
Before a cancerous battering fist
Fading away into history
Atom of dust in infinity.

So I prayed.

Still shape in mortuary foil
Fired to ash or rot into soil
Tumour monster inside of me
Sabotage of all I wanted to be.

So I prayed.

Of Galilee blood, golden hair
He entered my mind, don't know from where
His voice was the wind
But it was warm and true
And he said: 'My child I shall always love you.'

Back from icy brink of death
From numbing chill of reapers breath
Staring up at a hospital ceiling
But now at blue skies of healing.

In heavenly oceans was I bathed
It was because of Christ I was saved
No longer in pain, no longer distraught
And that is a miraculous thought.

Take It Like a Man

Woman here I am
A passionate man
Romantic to the extreme
Lovingly keen.

Erotica, nirvana
Xanadu, Karma Sutra
Take as much time as you can
But take it like a man.

We've spent a long time
Putting it off
Making excuses and delays
But surely now it's about the right time
To explore different ways.

Arabians and Japanese
Supposedly have good fun
Whereas Europeans
Have staid routines
And lovemaking is humdrum.

So like I say
Let's get love underway
In bedrooms of infinite sun.

Time

Time's a great healer
Some people say
Yet things often worsen
With each passing day,
Some also add
That life is too short
But not if it's dingy
Sad and distraught.
Some people look at
The clock all day
Waiting for things to get underway.
Others don't bother about time at all
For it waits for no one
And death gets us all.

Thatcher

Community smasher
Union basher
Moral fibre
The decider.

Privatisation
Incarceration
Frustration
Demoralization.

Industrial executioner
Miners' persecutor
Policing the weak
Of those who can't speak.

Rising crime
Short sharp shock
Disguised junta
Superior stock.

No such thing as society
Only individuals to blame
Poor and sick the losers
Profit the name of the game.

Void

Cannot describe infinity
By science or divinity
Or any possible dimension
It's outside my comprehension.

It would seem only death
Is the passport to
An understanding outside me and you.

A place which exists
Outside of time
Inconceivable to humankind,
Cannot be seen
Cannot be heard
Cannot be touched
By mortal concerns.

Kingdom of the soul
Immortal blood
Everything lasts forever
As eternity should.

Under the Sand

Lakes of the stuff
Petrol dollar treacle
Financial greed
For business people
Oily money
Oily hands
Dripping evil.
Lubrication for a human race
That needs the stuff
For modern life to take place
To run efficiently, smoothly together
It's a poison we might
Need to drink forever.
But when it runs out
And wells are dry
And no more smoke climbs into the sky
Our machinery will seize, cough
Stand still
And the world of the wheel
Will be terminally ill.

The Firm

Wanna Mercedes or Rolls Royce?
Or a Jag? Take your choice
What about a big cigar
You're part of the firm
One of us you are.

We are respectable businessmen
Who mean no harm nor to cause alarm
Just to collect our fees
For client protection
LSD and Amphetamines.

How about listening in to our talks
About Mafia links
And corruption of sorts,
About how we run the entire world
Respectably of course –
We honour our word.

Sparrows Patience

Doesn't swoop, dive nor wheel
Just hops humbly around a field
Or fence or hedgerow
Maybe someone's lawn
Into humility the sparrow was born.

Peaceful patience
No talons nor claws
No carrion nor prey
Nor hunting for a cause,
Just worms and the bread
That someone kind throws
To the common sparrow
That everyone knows.

Sad Songs

Laments and regrets
Sorrows and upsets
Bills and debts
Heartbreaks and mistakes,
Things that go wrong
Are all in this song.

Often it's the rain
We find ourselves in
Wandering to and fro
From tears to laughter
Then back to tears
Through life we sadly go.

I knew a man who was very old
A far wiser person than I
He said sometimes
You can cry all your life
Inside so really deep down.

You wander through a city
Late at night
You hear your footsteps below
You'd love to know if there is a God
But he never seems to show.

You know your life is ticking away
In a countdown to heaven knows where
You smile at a stranger who could be a friend
But they, like many others, don't care.

Space Undertaker

He's the man
In the cosmic van
Digging graves
In deepest space.

He's the one
The slick machine
Who arranges burials
In sector sixteen.

He's the guy
Who travels so fast
From shroud to shroud
Of graveyards vast.

He's the worker
Who does double shifts
Outside of time
If any exists.

But it's just a job
And he's a slave
Digging closer
Towards his own grave.

Snakes Mirror

Coiled intertwining
Slit eyes shining
Twisted scales of hell
Snakes mirror will tell.
Sees a victim unaware
Rushes lethally over to where
A message is delivered
Of hissing breath
As the mirror reflects
The slithering death.

Love and Hate

Caring?
Sharing?
Feeling?
Loving?
Touching?
Confiding?
Supporting?

Suspicion?
Indecision?
Lust?
Distrust?
Resisting?
Persisting?
Not listening?

Uncle Sam's Cafe

We got coffee, candy, coke, burgers
Officially granted CIA murders,
Looking back we don't give a damn
About napalm burned kids in Vietnam.
Our B52s dropped an urgent message –
Don't mess with Uncle Sam's power fetish
Just look up at the sky as in 1945
When people of Hiroshima got blinded, fried.

We've got the very latest
In combating crime
It's a place of total surveillance time
More jails to keep locked up the danger
More electric chairs, gas chambers.
A place of opportunity free and humane
Providing you always lose the game.

Call in at the cafe anytime you're free
This land of plenty, democracy.

Lunardrift

Scarecrows just standing there
In a world which doesn't care
Crying across the darkened miles
In wasted breath of exile.

Barred windowsill – a world out there
Past walls, locks, barbed wire
Recollections of once being free
Being what they wanted to be.

Madness is not what normal must be
So wire them up for some ECT
Asylum pylon of a million volts
Of therapeutic thunderbolts.

Psychiatric stereotype
Boris Karloff on a moonlit night
Deranged, deadly, wielding a knife
Lock all doors and windows tight.

He's coming now – the bogeyman
Keep as still and silent as you can
Foaming mouth like a raging sea
He's not what human ought to be.

Hospital grounds, drinking from a fountain
Understanding them is like climbing a mountain
Without any hands or feet
Hard to comprehend when minds don't meet.

Flying High

Look at those astronauts
Circling the sun
Now they're coming back down
Telling tales of having had fun.
They glimpsed Earth from so far away
A blue jewel lit by the sun's rays
They saw red rusts of Martian canals
They were kissed by Venus
Whilst space storms howled,
They were outrun by Mercurian wings
Rockets had problems with suspension springs
Oxygen levels had run quite low
They told us so much we didn't know.
But now they're happy
Back home
Away from Jupiter's rain
And interstellar strain
Eating fish and chips
Life on Earth they love to bits.

Whitehall Asylum

Salt of the earth
Of heroes gone
Falling down in world war one
Blood and fire
Lives tangled and mangled
In barbed wire.
Machine gun chatter
Of lethal conversation
Spilling bloody pints
Of a young generation
Straight from school
Rushed into hell,
Politicians stayed at home
Safe and well.
Some day someone
Should write a book
About war torn faces
Stuck in the muck
Broken bodies
Blood and gas
Killing all guarantees
Reason has.

What the Dead Said

They spoke of peace
No more demands
From somewhere so wonderful
In distant lands
Of a walk down corridors
Of eternal light
No longer prisoners of the night.
They drank from a cup
The sweetest of wine
It all opened up
No worries about time
No problems, sorrow, sadness or pain
New minds and bodies refreshed by the rain.

Vietnam

A messy sort of war
Left up in the air
Uncle Sam pulled out
Leaving everyone nowhere.

Landmines still
Waiting to blow off feet
Napalm scorched faces
Of flamethrower heat.

Craterland, wasteland
Bleaker than the moon
Starker, darker
Apocalypse soon.

One legged people
Land of the blind
Unable to get
What they cannot find.

Eagle Eye

Telescopic vision
As high as the sun
Swoops into the night
As the day is done,
Feathered devil
Diving so fast
From the heavens
Down to earth at last.
Sees all, misses nothing
Trusts the wind
And its own cunning,
Puts faith in its talons
And remarkable eyes
Taking thousands of snapshots
From deep in the skies.

Far Away Places

Can we go further
Than this earth
A holiday really our
Money's worth,
Out in the reaches
Of deepest space
Where other suns shine
In a far better place,
Where there's lots of peace and quiet
Away from cars, fast food and riots
Away from politicians and pushy people
Corrupt regimes and all that's evil.
Mars seems the best bet
But Venus is nice
Or to chill out on Pluto
Which is solid with ice,
But wouldn't it be better
If we could remain
On wonderful earth
Without problems and pain.

Broken Machines

Everything seemed to be going right
We put left foot forwards
Then the right
Onwards moving towards a goal,
Then suddenly appeared a gaping hole.

The path had widened
Of our mistakes
Until the ground began to shake
A hurricane hit us by surprise
We sank so deep in our demise.

Wining and Dining

Here's to our relationship
Candlelit dinner to crown it
Toast to romantic dreams
When fantasy is what it seems.
Your eyes meet mine
I return a glance of affection
And my heart starts to burn
In anticipated combustion
Where I love you such
There's not enough air
And our loving's too much
For anywhere,
And when the guests have gone
I say I love you
That I can actually
Prove it to you
In the here there and now
And of course it's so urgent
We don't need to wonder how.

Cloudy (Head Full of Tears)

I remember as a child
My mother always smiled
Despite a hard working day
A life often difficult
With not much fun
But she never moaned in dismay.

And what did I do
The smarty pants kid?
I achieved a bare fraction
Of what my parents did
I read text books
Did my 'A' levels
Felt so clever
And in smugness I revelled.

And now as I sit
In my asylum room
I realise that very soon
I must do something real
Make a sad soul smile
Or phone someone
I've neglected for a while.
For all qualifications
That I have amassed
Have so little worth
And I'm completely outclassed
By giants of unselfish humanity
As my mother and father will always be.

Day Became Night

Eclipse because of this
What's done and been said
Only ourselves to blame
For the oncoming dread.
On television
A Whitehouse politician
Announces all may soon be night
After they launch a nuclear strike.
Communications paralysed
In devastation
With nowhere to hide,
Radiation will creep
Into all we've known
A burning shell
Of a once green home,
Wastelands left from the blast
Replacing the dream that didn't last.

Director Dan

I'm Dan the businessman
Making as much money as I can
On a roller coaster of profit
So good I'm never stepping off it.

In my company Jag in a traffic jam
Lights go red to green and I'm off again
Accelerating towards endless consumption
Dying in a glory of production destruction.

Mergers of greed, blood and oil
Workers coffins of lightweight foil
Cemeteries of millions broken by the wheel
Suicide system of unfeeling steel.

December

Icicles of an iron maiden
Pierce me deep inside
Usurp any remaining warmth
Last night I dreamed I died.

This is no season for singing birds
But a time of frozen ground
Where damp faces press
Against windows so cold
And snowflakes deluge down.

Cars marooned on blocked up roads
Icy inertia like frozen toads
A kids face gazing into a shop
Of all those toys he hasn't got.

The badger lies deep
The fox asleep
The cold creeps through
The cracks in you.

Brew some tea
Make some toast
Wrap up well, cover ears the most
Prepare to fight this winter chill
Miss the flu, avoid being ill.

Lamps of Midnight

Lamps sway, swing
Deliriously, sickening:
Who are these men
Gunfighters close on our tracks
Will they creep up and shoot us
In our backs?
Will they surround us
With a message of death
Of gun-smoking barrels
Of vindictive breath?

Or are they aliens
Suddenly arrived
Who can only take over
If we're no longer alive,
Is that disc in the sky
A craft from afar
From their doomed planet
Amidst the stars?

Should we speak
Announce ourselves
Or run like mercury
To the hills,
Who are these holders of the lamps
Closing in on us now
Thick and fast?

Dimension

Often people say
They cannot grasp
The notion of space without end
They feel something must always
Be further afield
And that idea
They can't comprehend.

But that's a basic mistake
In a blameless way
Because we're schooled
To think of quantity
But the whole essence
Of conceptualising space
Is to get away from
Ideas of infinity.

For it's not about distance
Of things to be measured,
It's more a dimensional thing
Which eludes us forever
But if it didn't
Earth would be a drab place
Having had removed
It's enigma of space.

Haunted

Screech of a bat
Squeal of a mouse
Haunted like hell
Is this house,
Bodies under floorboards
In the garden, in the walls
Late at night
A distressed ghost calls.
No owner has lasted
More than three weeks
All got petrified
Became insane or died
Icy atmosphere
Staircase of blood
This house is evil
Within it no good.

House of Machines

Microwave timer says it's ready
Alarm clocks wake me up
Answerphone is waiting
There's no time left on my own.
Videotape is rewound
Mobile phone rings too
Dishwasher has finished its cycle
Cake mixer exactly on cue.
The house is ticking, buzzing, clicking,
Full of bleeps and whines
It's all too true
It's a mechanical zoo
With robots around all the time.

Exclusive

The cloakroom is by the stairs
Nobody allowed with beards, long hair,
We employ a bouncer if all else fails
We have a salon to manicure nails.

I've a tanning booth at home you know
I watch my bank balance grow and grow
By thirty I should be a millionaire
As regards poverty I don't really care.

Wait a minute – my mobile phone's bleeping
I should be at home now sleeping
Or scanning columns of the *Financial Times*
Reading shrewdly between the lines.

For profit is God
And I'm his son
The corporate dynamo
The fastest one
Of mountains of money
Reaching into the stars
I might invest in Venus
Or consider buying Mars.

Nothing can stop me
My wallet's too big
My suit so expensive
I'm sweating like a pig
My Rolex says it's half past nine
Yet I can't buy love nor any more time.

Institutionalisation

A sickness not wished for
But foisted upon
Through containment in places
As years grind on.
Same old faces
Same old place
Old routines
Staring into space.

The clock the ruler
Who signals time
For events as we queue
In obedient lines,
Night medication
Last mug of tea
Losing touch
With what it means to be free.

Fumes of a Life

Smoke holds his soul
Tight as it rolls
Into urban skies,
Of a factory destined life.

Forty years on a machine
Pay packet Friday
Pub Saturday
Working Men's Club Sunday
Shockwave Monday,
The machine again.
Bad chest, lungs eaten
Canteen cuppas, stale cake
Back out through the gates
Siren blowing an end to today
To start again the next day.
He's invisible now
A thought in a few minds
He'd had no joyride
It was a difficult life
Spread now in atoms
A billion-fold
And skies above cry
As his story is told.

Hurt

Across the room
I saw you crying
And whilst you did
Inside I was dying,
Then in the train
I heard your voice
The grief gave me pain
And I made a choice.

Decided to go back to you
Do all the things we used to do
All the good times of moments bright
Forget sad, lonely trains in the night.

Off the platform to kiss your eyes
Of salty tears of springtime skies
So sorry having hurt the one I loved
All around me below and above.

Have They Given Us Up?

How long now in innermost keeps
Of castles of madness where we sleep
Of dungeons lit with ridicule
Of a public view we're crazy fools.
Why are we left in the Netherworld
Of eclipsed fortune stale and cold
The tunnel of vision without any light
Out of mind out of sight.

Will we ever walk the fields again
City streets in showers of autumn rain
Are we locked in a stalemate always to be
No thoughts no moves to set us free.
Is our fate a stamp of ignorance
Of being denied a second chance
Of fading away old and grey
Misunderstood for all our days?

LA Cop

Codes a genius couldn't crack
Powerful pistol
Strapped to his back
The one who catches
The cleverest crooks
In his own style
Not by the official books.
The one on his own
At loggerheads with his boss
Disillusioned hero
Who doesn't give a toss
Has seen society go to rack and ruin
Goes right in with bullets shooting.
The one on the margin
Who sees through it all
Who jacks in the job
Because of all
The hypocrisy, bribes and
Double dealing
Deep down a cop's life
Is a bitter flavoured feeling.

Cities

Buildings comprise
Blind steel eyes
Taxi rank sharks
Of tungsten hearts.

Where is the shire horse
That stamped at the junction
We thought community was eternity
We killed it for modernity.

A transistor with its back removed
The sprawling metropolis leaves us unmoved
Frozen in our passion
Angry with the deal
Of a world of calculation
Where we no longer feel.

Vanquished the moon and gone the stars
Our children machines, our Gods our cars
The tower of Babel is nearly complete
But we find no heaven, only hell do we meet.

Atheists Prayer

I do not believe in the divine
I worship only a scientific shrine,
Heaven is a word not a place
Darwin was right about the human race.

A rocket is progress
A cross regression
Disasters are natural
Man is biological succession.

The microscope means more to me
Than Christ and immortality
The computer is my one and only God
Einstein holds the divining rod.

I pay no homage to chapel or church
But devote my life to atomic research
See matter and chemicals as life's foundation
And evolution the cause of our creation.

It Rained Forever

Sodden fields
Rain soaked eagles
Ladybirds drowned
Starlings marooned,
Gushing gutterings
Rivers bursting their banks
Crying clouds
Heartbroken skies.
Steamed up windows
Flooded world
Torrential tears
Long dripping days,
Somewhere dry
We all must find
Away from oceans
Of saturated minds.

Icy Nights

Lumpy frozen thoughts
My pillows tonight
Cold dreams of yesteryear
I'm tucked in tight
Praying for the morning
Calling for the sun
To banish icy exile
Once my penance is done.

When will this winter be over
Dark nights of deaf waves
When will somebody say it's summer
And time no longer hurt me this way?

January

Back end of Xmas
Anticlimax time
Cold and drab
As we stand in a line
Outside the Post Office
To get giros cashed
Xmas spending
Nearly broke our backs.

Slushy pavements
Slushy trains
Slushy conversations
Slushy brains.
Slushy attitudes
Slushy minds
Dreaming of spring and summertime.

Just Like Any Other Day

Same routine
Same scene
Similar faces
Familiar places
Shades of grey
Nothing new to say
Same old tea breaks
Same old mistakes
Same cars on the roads
Same bark of a dog next door
Same Sunday church bell tones
Same sanctuary of our homes
Same cold morning
Same dark night
Same waves lapping
Same birds in flight,
Is it all instinctive
What goes on
And if life was any different
Would it all be wrong?

Broken

Sometimes at night
I see you edge
Around the foot of my bed
Your ghost returning
To break my heart
The end was only the start.

Why did you leave me
So long ago
To drive lonely roads
I really don't know,
Left to wander
Oceans and skies
Seeing your face
Through misty eyes.

You died just as the sun came out
Upon this world
Into my heart,
Now only fear speaks
Of sorrowful days
The sun's died too
And heaven's been razed.

Spanner in Blue

Semi skilled operative
Has grease in his mind
At the end of the day
When he tries to unwind.

Being chained to machines
Gives mechanical dreams
The factory siren
Sees him wake up frightened.

Each day the same bus
Same factory floor
Same workmates, same tea breaks
Demands repetition yet more.

What remains is his wife
To come home to each night,
Is he really so different from me and you
The industrial slave of the spanner in blue.

Blacktrack

Siberian sleigh
Of a lonely locomotive
Cutting its way
Through the expanse
Thousands of miles of whitened wonder
Tracks like a red hot lance.
The engines heart is beating
In it's love of frozen air
Everywhere amidst snow from above.
Dotted stations
Like currants afloat
In a whitened lake
Of continental milk,
Beleaguered figures
Overcoated, cold,
Bearded, intense
Young and old,
Waiting, waiting
For that train
Black track on white
Of Siberian plain.

When My Grandmother Died

Whilst she lived
Birds would warble
Dance from twig to twig
Hop from leaf to leaf,
And the long Summer
Secure, safe, mellow around us
Smiled.
'Life's alright
So long as you don't weaken,' she said.
When she died
Fields of flowers
Shrivelled up,
Birds fell from the trees,
Plummeting defunct,
I cried, cried and cried
Couldn't stop crying;
And I found myself weakening.

.

Tomorrows Tomb

It seems
We sing
Sad songs
These days
Of a green land we once knew
And good things we used to do
Before gardens became graveyards
Bones became dust
And political robots
Minds turned to rust.

Fictitious tales of care and love
Written in mushrooms rising above
Smoking stories of cremated ruin
Arsonists of our own undoing.

Oceans turned to ashtrays
Countries to sand
Days became nights
We forever damned.

Crying ghosts cannot forget
A funeral of a future
Of radioactive regret,
Wandering to and fro
Within four walls of hell
Your own burning body
All you can smell
On your gravestone
Of hallucinated shame
All you see
Is your own faded name.

Summer was a mellowness
Fresh air, cool sea
Life and love
For you and me;
Now it is winter
We are statues of stone
Meaning next to nothing
And nowhere is our home.

The Robot that Forgot

Straightforward delivery
Operating efficiently
Metallic womb
Too fast, too soon,
Dials register wisdom potential
Clone conformity mandatory, essential.
Mechanical dialogue
Intercom minds
Electric light for sunshine
Hiding behind blinds.
Computer future, aluminium creature
Science the bible, money the preacher.
Huddled before the TV
Where once was grass is now machinery,
Over the world falls acid rain
We rust but feel no guilt, no pain:
We no longer remember, we forgot to ask,
Queuing with you for the next mindless task.

The Home on the Hill

Drainpipes spew out the filthy weather
Red brick philanthropy of Victorian endeavour,
See them laughing or crying in the rain
In Asylum anoraks, forsaken all the same.
Cold linoleum corridors
Jangling keys, bolted doors,
The thin line of madness – ever so fine
If you overstep it you could lose a lifetime;
A language of secrecy, straightjacket minds
Freemasonry lunacy, insane signs.
And beyond the gates of gargoyled stone
And iron tougher than mortal bones
Are fields of freedom
Begging for the seeds
Of love watered by the madman's needs.

Gathering Ice

Snowmen wage war with the sun
Children tumble from a toboggan
The sky like lead with a blocked up head
Of yet more snow to come.

Whitened moors of winter footprints
Of sinking lovers' feet
Meandering romantically, even haphazardly
Hand in hand back home.

The approaching evening sees a welcome yellow glow
Of warmly switched on lights
And blinds shutting out searching snowflakes
Of December's frozen nights.

The badger lies still in woodland deep
In bedrooms of innocence children sleep
Outside the midnight hour is cold
The young so far from growing old.

Voices from churches slip into the skies
Soft smoke from chimney pots drifting high
Tolling bells and bright faces unite
Those gathering hope, gathering ice.

The Winter That Never Came

Metaphors though beautiful
Cannot conceive
But can give flesh to bone
They can help plant life
In burning deserts
Where before only death has grown.

My father?
Why yes! I knew him well
Used to play drums in my bedroom,
Give him hell,
Annoy him with the latest
Teenage fad
But through and throughout
I loved my dad.

Rambling through the mush of frozen woods
Or sharing the sight of warm spring buds
We played what seemed an immortal game
Now he's gone and the dice drowned in the rain.

Where is he now
That wonderful man
In some garden I wonder
In an unknown land?
Is he still of this world
Or much further away?
I would like to think
He will always stay.

Used to complain about the cold a lot
But never blamed others no matter what
And then in the heat of an August sunrise
He didn't open his eyes.

A Universal fact – everyone's father dies
But to each a unique cross to bear –
Such a precious part of our lives.
Oceans of fields and poppies a million-fold
Lie before my feet
I stroll through a world
More lonely than before
But in the end I hope we meet.

The last day of summer
Blew a wind so chill
Could well have been December
Never was my heart
Rammed so full of ice
And complacency torn asunder.

And yet!
Just as the storm
Was creeping in
With frosty etch
On mortal skin
The sun like a glory lit up the world
And winter failed to take him.

Cinders

Goodbye Brontosaurus
Disappeared from this world's stage
Crystallized for coal consumers
Of an electrical, technical age.

Until the ice you did your best
Till fossilized time left you dispossessed.

Bequeathed to the mind of humankind
Pyres of ancient extinction
Beacons of testimony to that fact
Flaming in industrial combustion.

Cretaceous kings of earthshaking roar
Wiped out along with their children
A million years on plundered and mined
Sifting through chimneys of buildings.

Until the ice you did your best
Till fossilized time left you dispossessed.

Could Tyrannosaurus see what was to be
What an energy crisis required?
Incineration of both body and soul
Commercially, impersonally fired.

No thanks from all the profiteers
Just an assessment of energy trends
Cost balance sheets of those dead in the swamps
Statistics of means towards ends.

Farewell to the Fair

Remember the day the pylon crashed
Upon complacent roofs
And the reservoir of incubated hate
And accumulated muck much to our distaste
Fertilised our thoughts in its murky flood
Of what it was all about.
Teatime was great
With its sandwiches of steel
It's thermos of oil
In the world of the wheel,
Then our watches declared
That we must move on,
A blackbird was heard – we were deaf to its song.
With eyes of Apaches
Detecting the smoke of mushrooms
Rising from cities of sand
We still loved the lights and rides and stalls
Of a self made prison of twentieth century walls.
Sick and dizzy walking back through the night
The nuclear flask having captured our sight
As future generations unknowingly sleep
Lay in funfair wombs of a nightmare deep.
Whilst on a hill nailed to some wood
Was a man who shouted through a mouth of blood,
We laughed then rammed a spear in his side,
The black sky broke
And our only chance died.

Buttons for the Blind

The time is the evening
Funeral of our fun
All earth is burning
Like a suicidal sun;
Staring up at the flash
With foreshortened breath
Media headlines scriptures of death.

Astronauts of genocide bizarre
Who drove around dreams
In big black cars,
Worshipped weaponry shrines
Cutting into the clouds
Guaranteeing cremation
In nuclear shrouds.

Left peace on pacific atolls marooned
Scarred the face of reason
With confusion festooned,
Played Russian roulette
In zero sum style
Gambled everything away
Till nothing survived,
Only ashy cities, desert seas
And smoking skeletons of you and me.

Run of the Mill

Carry on reading
Don't lower your spectacles
Carry on eating
Don't let your food go cold,
It's just a passing body
Of little significance
Trudging down an endless road.

A train in the night
A ship out at sea
Important in themselves
But in a wider context, dull,
Like us, striving throughout our lives
To escape homogeneity
And say: 'This is me.'

But run of the mill we are
Each and every one
Our paths predestined
Before we left the womb,
Struggling through the years
Beneath the watchful sun
Fighting tears of acceptance
As the road winds on.

Signs of the Times

Has his tea at bang on five
Has a shave and a shower
Says he's glad to be alive
Keeps complaining of double vision,
Caused by delusions of too much television.

In a dusty drawer
Lie his dead father's war medals,
But he thinks he's even better
Because he's got four 'A' levels.

Yet on the day of his divorce
To his telephone,
He will reel with awe
And decide to open that drawer
For his achievements in life are none,

He will rejoin his dad
In a world which is sad
And father and son will be one.

The Block

Why should humanity have to exist
In a concrete compound where drainpipes twist
A slum in the heart of city centre gloom
Lit disinterestedly by an indifferent moon.

There's a burglary going on in room number four
And a baby battered by a whore next door
And as you mount the steps
There's a stench of meths
Drunk by a pensioner who gets depressed.

But just to whom can the residents pray
When even God turns away?

Rainy Day in Town

Winter suns lemon shafts
Reflections on cobbles
On a high street of
Dampened grey,
Figures huddled in a shop door entrance
Beleaguered in rivulets of rain.
Thunder cracked clouds
Lightning set skies on fire
Boiled the rain
Hit the old church spire.
Evening visitations
Of moistened breath
Midwinter's icy kiss of death,
Incessant urination driving down
In soddenness of dampness
A drowned, black town.

Guilty

Murder me for money
Take all I've got
It's all so hopelessly on fire now
So much have we lost.
Earth sickly spinning
Incandescently obscene
Our world we betrayed
Once clean, fresh and green.

It makes no difference
To speak with regret
Guilt is something
Any fool likes to forget,
The nuclear computer
Prints out your days
On death row you'll be
On death row you'll stay.

Auschwitz

Have those ovens
Really cooled down
After fifty years
On the dole?
Will grief of relatives
Ever end
Over loved ones
Who died in that hole?
A monument built by a madman
Who wished an empire
For a thousand years
He turned on taps
No one can turn back
Of a holocaust
Of oceans of tears.

Gone

Never so cold as now,
A fire in the grate
Burning itself out;
Sweet wrappers, freshness
Strangely absent
In this sickly heat, medicinal smell.

Unopened cards of 'Get Well Soon'
Pile up
As mother makes tea
For one whilst another unused cup
Smashes her to bits
The very sight of it.

A storm is coming
Cracking clouds
Into a conclusion,
Fiery bolts only ricochet
Off roofs to no avail.

In the storm's zenith
A horrific calm.

Chain Smoker

Emptying machines
To satisfy his dreams,
Out of poisoned jaws
A curly wisp pours,
Must cut down –
But not today,
Tomorrow perhaps –
So far away.

Sixty sticks of suicide every day
Pleasantly smoking his life away.

Let's tension loose –
The classic excuse,
Teeth decay, lungs rot away,
A man's best friend
From start to tab end.

Sixty sticks of suicide every day
Pleasantly smoking his life away.

'Cool, deluxe, satisfying, mild,'
The manufacturers' brainwashed child,
Content to be a coughing slave
First in the queue for an early grave.

Jupiter

Gassy giant of methane fame
I shall always love you just the same
You turned me on when I first flew close
Saw your moon's bodies through coloured smoke.
It took so long to catch your eye
I, voluptuous Venus, far across the sky
My heart incandescently hot
I loved you with
All the heat I'd got.
Yet partings are sad
As endings often are
Your mightiness now
Just a winking star
You are lonely, icy, cold
In solitary orbit,
Sad, getting old.

Anthem for a Dead Man

Rain bathes the asylum
As I mount the steps,
Steps which seem blacker
Than the staircase of death,
'Your brother is dead,' the doctor said.
As the sheet unfurled
A face twisted in defeat
Said: 'I'm sorry,'
And a voice within me said: 'I am.'
Back down the steps
Past trains of hedgerows
Glistening in the rain I hobbled
With an agenda leading nowhere.
With insanity already stamped
Upon the grave, children sing songs
Of a man I knew
And a man who once knew me,
They sing of him
What they know and understand
Although they do not understand
What they know;
And as the nights
Grow blacker inside of me
There is a slow, switching off, of lights.

Sad

Reflections rising up from puddles of rain
And dripping show windows do the same
I see myself in the same old frame
Same old body, same old name.

The years take their toll of all of us
Wear us away like sea to a bay
Lonely little islands unseen, unknown
Through all our lives we try to own
A piece of this world something to hold
But it all slips away and we start to get old.

Like the flowers of a season
As sun is to summer
As wind is to spring
As snow is to winter
We stand in defence of our own domain
Of the garden of life till we fade and pale.

We try so hard to get somewhere
Go round and round on well worn ground
Walking through cities our sadness the same
Our tears coming down along with the rain.

Supertanker

Chip fat for your wife
Fuel for your bike
Hydrocarbon honey
For whatever you like.
Power for your car
Or a super strong tyre,
Supertanker shall retire
In a glory on fire.
Crossing all waters
Seven seas the same
Round trip to North Cape
Stopping point Bahrain.
See it break ice, cut water
No holding back, giving Neptune no quarter,
You'd better flee for your life
When I run aground
Poisoning seabirds for miles around
Painting black the sands
Of far away lands
Too much for one world
To hold in its hands.

Maimed Minds

Sane and insane
Who draws the line?
And who should serve
An indefinite time?

Brain deterioration
Starts stultification
Inhibits motivation
Breeds vegetation.

We don't know when we are going
The time may never come,
But one thing is pretty certain –
The damage is already done.

Robin

Braver than most
You like to boast
Come – eat crumbs from my hand
Fight Winter despite a losing race
No worms in this frozen land.
Sad to say it's a human world
With creatures squeezed out of it all,
Best to stay so very high
In your heaven of the sky.
Visit my window when you have time:
For your love of nature
Is a mirror of mine,
Your orange coat
Of softened glow
So warm, so good
Amidst the snow.

Red Sky Over Redcar

ICI stinking
But the people unblinking
Their courage forever afloat
Nostalgia trampled beneath dollars and yen
Of the sinking Redcar Boat.

Hopes wings have spread
The Phoenix has flown
Only returning
As redundancy payments are drawn,
Crypt of a skyline furiously red
People's pyre of a pride
Of good times long dead.

Shop steward flitting between
Drops of rain
From street to street
In recognized pain,
Execution at sunrise
Teessiders' tears
Of unemployed agony
Through bruised, battered years.

It's no joke
Multinational flooding
Breaching all dykes of hope,
Sand sifts through a young boy's hands
His dad's torn face
Is what profit demands.

Sandcastles on sunny days
Will not be built again.
No bucket and spade
Could ever measure the pain,
Just a sad waiting
For terminal dawn
A generation forsaken
As silicon kid is born.

Strangers

Ebbing eyesight in chlorine clouds
Sinking away in quagmire shrouds
Mowed down in mud by machine gunfire
Trapped and entangled in barbed wire;
Silent nights smashed as big guns fill
Bodies full of shrapnel in a crusade to kill.

Far away, politicians' glasses of port
Meet in a toast
To a war they've not fought,
Only planned, directed and idly discussed
Manufacturing hatred, engineering distrust
Trading clarity for confusion
In a ruthless power lust.

Only one thing in common
Do leaders share
With those on the battlefield
Falling down everywhere,
And that is their wine
Has good body and is red
Draining away forever
Like the blood of those dead.

Lament for an Aunt

When I was sad she
Would give me a thousand clowns.
When I did thirst she
Would give me an ocean.
Childhood games and chocolate cakes
Like some fabulous beast
Come rushing back
Into a mind
Humiliated in paying homage to time.

Whilst she breathed on this earth
Nature would swell
In ripe radiance of a smile
And even as she aged the shadow of death
In it's malice to hurt was futile.

The news was horrific thunder in the head
The seas dried up the land dull and flat
Sights of a swooping shadow unseen
Came and crucified the dream.

Bus

The coiled queue
Twists
In November mists
I await the bus
Like all of us.

Sunday afternoons
Sees the cleaning
Of cars
Polished by a class
Which is not ours.

Lying still
Within the mill
Grease and oil seep
Till we awaken
Machines from their sleep.

Unlike those of suburbs
We are confined
In city centres
Of metropolitan mind.

The chatter with which we begin the day
Is merely something to do and something to say
As we reflect of a bus to be on
I queue with you in nocturnal neon.

Down Through the Blue

Only the blues can a broken man sing
Of long lost hope and everything
Dreams marooned on alien cliffs
A biography lacking apparent motive.

An existence necessarily bound
To the treadmill of psychiatric ground
From icy confinement frozen flower
The pub, supermarket is his finest hour.

All those Autumns from behind a wall
His restless soul said: 'Free me.'
And his tortured ears heard uncertainty call:
'Does anyone believe me?'

Liberty was there at one time, yes,
But it went slipping and sliding away
And all he'd built was razed in a blight
Which festered in ugly decay.

Moonlight from the window crisscrossing the bed
Brings little solace or comfort
Shadows of shaking hands dance on the wall
His will is at breaking point.

Whence drops of water fused sea and sky
A life now circumscribed without sight
For this is his vision, his brave new world
Of endless days of night.

Earthbound Pilot

The earthbound pilot
With useless wings
Has so little time
As he downwards spins.

Thoughts of war
Flash through his head
And memories of comrades
Shot down long dead.

Forgive the enemy
But do not forgive me
Is his flying epitaph
As his thoughts flow free.

Shot down by the foe's
Still smoking gun
As his recollections rush
One by one.

Brutally Frank

My name's Frank
The Lord I thank
For a career tough as a tank
A prison officers job
Requiring a raucous gob
Manhandling the criminal sod.

Nice to kid myself
The job's demanding
Strutting power drunk
Up and down lepers landing
Swinging keys, feeling fine
Going right by the book
All down the line.

If they can't do the time
They shouldn't do the crime.

Always bullied in my younger years
Now it's my turn to cause a few tears
Twisting arms of convicted scum
Breaking them down, regretting they'd come.
Sadism dramatically evolves
Upon those whose hope
Its acid dissolves,
Those corrupt and locked up
On lepers landing
Deaf to reason, beyond all understanding.

If they can't do the time
They shouldn't do the crime.

Usually clocking off
Around about nine
But half past ten
If there's overtime,
I'm shattered
But it's something I love to do
The ego boost of the screw in blue.

It's the lifers
I most like breaking
The unofficial side
Of the job's undertaking
Beating ups out of sight
On the quiet
Batons and shields
At first sign of a riot.

At the end of the day
They'll find crime doesn't pay
Be it narcotics or robbing a bank
They'll learn the hard way
That's what I always say
Being brutal
Being brutally Frank.

Broken Wings

Spinning through space
Towards earthy embrace
In awaiting arms of doom
Youths of nineteen
With life so much unseen
In smashed up contraptions so soon.
Those who loved them
Of an impatience deranged
Telegram ears, seconds like years
Crying deep oceans
At war's twisted fist
Scarring air fodder faces
Which now don't exist.
Smoky spiralling
Of teenage mortal ruin
Debris of human economy
Berets of bloody plume.
Champagne in high places
But never quite so high
As sky torn visitations
Of those destined to die.
Their finest hour
Amidst bullet splintered glass
Of cockpit coffins
Flames and gas.
Flying as far as their bodies could stand
Lives slipping away like the finest of sand
Broken butterflies of a war effort command
Burning their names deep into the land.

Icarus

He was a man
Who tried to fly
Too high;
His wings melting in the sun,
Wings made from mortal wax.
Falling,
Falling,
Down to the land
Falling in a glorious way,
Down to the ground
Forever earthbound,
Soon to sink deep into clay.

Wastwater (Lake District)

Above ominous waters
Sharp scree projects,
Solitary flowers are
Strangled by the wind;
Once here a great battle was fought
In which life and love were slain.

Here only the voice of cruelty speaks
With witches enthroned on surrounding peaks,
Sending evil spells into steely grey skies
Never visit Wastwater whilst you still have eyes.

Behind the Wall

A nearby playground
Sees children's grins
Climbing higher on swings
And a roundabout spins;
Bad stories about those behind the wall
Told by a public of retributive call.

Then it starts to rain
And the kids go away
But the bogeymen they fear
Forever stay;
The roses in the grounds
Drink a rainy day of June
Then the anger comes like thunder
And a storm of sorrow too.

From behind the wall
Lies an impossible task:
To see what went wrong
And piece together the past,
Perhaps ten years have slipped away
A legacy of a crazy yesterday.

As evening falls
And curtains close
The weary children sleep
But behind the wall
A night of pain does befall
Those who can only weep.

Last Bus to Bedlam

Lights in the bus are spinning
Radiating rays of sepulchral madness
It's goodbye to posh cigarettes
I'll soon be rolling my own with the lads.

Again – those lights derangingly bright
Cutting into the night
Broadcasting to a cool and complacent world
That at last I've given up the fight.

That figure at the gate in a starched white coat
Resembles modification of the mind –
The psychological shredder we all go through
At some time or other in our lives.

'Get a room ready –
We've got one coming in,
Did you read it in the papers today?
Diminished responsibility
Requires psychiatric facility
Somewhere well out of the way.'

Money

Root of what the hell you are
Scorpion in my pocket
Stinging the years as my time disappears
Crawling through my wallet.

Financial vomit
Oozing,
Sickness of no cure
Dribbling down my shirt
I return to the dirt
The unforgiving exit door.

Cerebral wheels of insolvency
Of friction in my head
Lubricated in sugar daddy land
Bequeathed by the dissolute dead.

You metallic bastard
Chinking in my ears
Rattling me to madness
Of undeserved arrears,
Overdrawn tombstones
Looming in my eyes
Awakening in a till of a nightmare
Blackworld, bankrupt sunrise.

The robot of me
To obey and pay
Is all they want to see,
A credit card
Postpones the graveyard
Cheating fate
At least for today.

Love in a Cold Place

When I went down with flu
She said, 'I'll always love you,'
No matter how disabled or ill
She brought me broth and lemon squash
As I shivered with dizzying chill.

All the one night stands
In tropical lands
Only gave me VD
But now there's just one woman
Who is all I ever need
And she says all she needs is me.

It was in northernmost Sweden
When I bust my legs
On a crazy venture on ski's
That she looked after my cracked and broken bones
Washed my feet and bandaged my knees.

And when at last I could walk again
Through valleys of arctic spring
We filled the hours amongst wild flowers
And lakes reflected our loving.

I for so long frozen out in the cold
A refugee in search of the sun
And your love for me removed the agony
Of being alone and undone

The heat of our love melted ice of the earth
Never again would blizzards exist
So long as we lived, so long as we loved
Together amongst mountains and mist.

Burger Murder

Orwell's farm
Transplanted in time
Scintillating sheen
Of Formica canteen.
Trapped between bread
A bovine deathbed
Tomato sauce shrouds
For cosmopolitan crowds.
Burgers by the billion
Boost the balance sheet
Of commercialised homicide
On those who can't speak.
Gone earthy fragrance of farmyard shit
Revolving round a stainless steel spit
Images of feathered friends
Cooked, long dead
In cholesterolized bellies of those well fed.
Echoes of farewell
As the truck drove away
Down dusty lanes
To the motorway
To the slaughterhouse
Turned upside down
Hacked and dismembered
Fried crispy gold brown.
No daylight only twilight neon
Cool rain on a green field all long gone
Funeral on a plastic plate
Knife and fork sealing fate
Chewed to oblivion without visible trace
Just a belch and grease on someone's face.
Old MacDonald's shopping around

Buying his hens the best batteries in town
Fattening pills and protein boosters
For next on death row's condemned roosters.
Denied defence
Denied a trial
Denied a life
Through cages they file
Never ending extermination;
Hitler in comparison
Was an angel.

Living Like a Lighthouse

Whoever said only children are spoilt
Could not be further from the truth
Lonely days playing records in a bedroom
Or tears in early years are proof.

A thousand Sunday empty afternoons
Whilst mum and dad sat reading the papers
And an only child alone on the back garden lawn
Deprived of brothers and sisters.

For me it seemed particularly bad
I wonder – was it for others too?
The bondage only to a mum and a dad
And nobody else to love you.

Excited little boys at the corner shop for sweets
Or pony tailed girls with hair plaited neat
Was the closest I got to other childhood kin
There was so much to give but it remained within.

To have shared a birthday with a sister's smile
To have grown up with another child
Would have taken the acid out of my eyes
And let me see blue instead of grey skies.

It suffices to say we got splashed by the spray
Of callous waves in our early days,
Because the last thing we ever
Wanted to be was exiled out
In an unfeeling sea
Talking to ships of impersonal iron
And deaf oceans beneath cold stars of Orion.

The Blue Tit

Black, blue, yellow, green
Pigments of a feathered queen,
Now that her work is past
And her heart can rest at last.

Her mate – never really far away
Dancing on the acorns of a nearby tree
Singing in the sunshine, drinking the dew
Though his days of pleasure are few.

A bag of nuts swinging in space –
A gift from the human race,
Warmly appreciated, for only birds know
The killer wind of winter, its remorseless snow alive.

So go ahead little bird, enjoy life while you can
Till nature's horn calls you again,
For then you build nests and wearily fly
Many miles each day to keep your children.

Lighthouse

Has saved many a ship
From floundering on the rocks
As it braves the waves
And disaster it mocks.

Could tell a great story
Of boats in their glory
As it shires through the gloom;
A sentinel of Neptune.

The Future Was

The future was bought
By trading our dreams
Peace had its price
In our space machines
Enough thrust got us from A to B
With vision cloudy we could not see
Turned to clay from radiation's wand
We conjured our cities into sand.

Our rockets went in circles
Of a graveyard vast
Lessons learned were burned
Along with the past.

The quest uncertain
The means unknown
From acorns of ignorance
Experience had grown
And somewhere near the sun
We began to dive
And our future
Like a shooting star
Burned out through the skies.

The Child and the Tree

Oh! Tree you are tired
Worn out, expired,
Kids have carved their names
In your spine,
Tell me tree – just between
You and me
What in life have you most admired?
I would like to think
It is all you have seen –
Bare Winter branches
Or Springs leaves of green
Or the little boy
Who made a tree den
In your bones of branches as his playground home.
The child loves you,
He always sees you as young,
A sapling glistening in
Curtains of rain,
Not crooked or wizened but with a
Future so full, live in hope young tree
As this child has done.

After This

Death's sidekick of time
Creeps into our homes
Turns us into history
Faded memories and bones,
Faces become fossils forgotten
Stuck in museums glass eyed and rotten.
Eras of triumph, shining cities in the sun
Slide into dissolution
Tombstones they become,
Signposts of the ages
Saying we did this and that
And the future was what
We were aiming at.
All that we knew, all that we had
All that was good, all that was bad
Was in our eyes raining onto the land
As everything solid crumbled to sand.
Drowned, burned, poisoned, shot
Or the three score and ten,
Is that it?
Our lot?
Mummified, mortified,
Do we ever come back
To the world we walk out of
In a storm cold and black?

Away

And sometimes he wishes
He didn't wake up
To face more empty grey days,
Kicking off his shoes
Crashing out on the bed
He enters an unconscious daze.

Where is the wife he loved so much
And rushed home from the factory to meet
Where are the kids he once conceived
That ran around his feet.

Wars, weddings, births, hills
Demands repetition yet more
A wardrobe of clothing a generation
Out of date; sleep helps him shut the door.

Nothing now is novel or new
All played out, pleasures so few
Another cigarette helps him forget
Things he knows that he should regret.

Wearily he prays to a God
In whom he's always had faith
That tonight he might depart forever
From earth towards a far better place.

Wings of a Day

Summer in its drunkenness
Of thickened air
Shouted through the evening
To a child unaware
'Come, see life eclipsed in a day,'
As the sun warmed the meadow
Of ripe rickets of hay.
The butterfly flitting through thistles
Of purple lush
Settling on a nettle
Beneath a blackberry bush.
Sad, because time was fast closing in,
The child, again unaware,
Watched with a grin.
River-like, remorseless watery chant,
Solemn procession of sunlit slant,
Shrieking kingfisher, mockingbird hum,
Cruel connotations of a funeral drum.

Evening shadows lengthening,
Dark taking hold
Of a lackadaisical day
And a butterfly old,
The child so young, going home to sleep
With a Summer's day memory drowsy, deep;
Evening phosphorescence
Sweeping rays across fields,
The blackberry bush a pathetic shield.
Only a sinking sunset witnessed the sight
And prayers of all creatures
Sifted through the night.

When Shadows Stay

Little boy plays
With soldiers in a fort
It's a birthday present
His Granddad bought.
Pieces of plastic planted here and there
Granddad smells acrid shell shocked air.

Little lad sipping cherryade
Granddad sees a bloody fusillade,
Warm, sticky smoking blood
Killing love as wicked wars should.

Sprawled on the carpet
By the lounge fire,
The plastic pieces are soldiers, every one,
No pieces of politicians
With which to have fun.
Only grey and green figures
Of conscripted brown,
Faces in the mud
Gassed, shot down.

Flanders Fields
Now fresh with flowers,
Gone the carnage of clashing powers.
Gone the gunfire
Rats around the feet
Chewing toes and ankles
For something to eat.

Gone the bloodbath
Which drained away
With hate and horror
On Armistice Day.
Gone the young men
Who died crying for their mothers
Blown to bits with countless others.
Rotting skeletons beneath the flowers
Of names forgotten
Within a matter of hours.

Yet quagmire burials
Do not exist
For fallen down heroes
Of battlefield mist.
No graveyard ever contains
Such priceless souls
Of precious remains.

They will go on breathing
As young as ever before
Untouched by evil of a crazy war.
Be it 1916
Or the child playing today
Nothing can take those soldiers away.

Reflections

Looking in a mirror
Am I ill?
Walking down the street
Of accusing, pointing fingers
Of those saying:
'He was in an asylum, you know.'

Is it not time
I climbed out of this slime
Bathed myself in sanity
Contacted reality
Dried my tears
And faced up to the remaining years?

I Died Yesterday

Is it really so
I once lived below
On that blue green world?
It seems so long ago.

I see it now
As a passing second
Where I became
What time beckoned
Glad to sad
Warm to cold
A child in a man
Who became so old.

Forgotten Song

When the blackbird
Fell off the guttering
It's choked clarity stuttering
Skies turned blue to black
The song went away
Never came back.

When the little girl
Pressed piano keys of melodies
The world's windows
Opened to that song
But now that girl is gone.

When every single living thing
Opened vocal chords to sing
And sunshine filled
The darkest places
We felt our time
Would not run races.

But it did.
It put wings upon
Our happiest times
Chased our moments
Hurried up our lives
Sang saddest of songs
To make us cry
Left us all wondering why.

Last Thoughts

Well I suppose my life
Or anybody's for that matter
Is a mixture of this and that
Thin experience which grows fatter.

I've tried that way
I've turned it round
Seen it from another side
But at the end of it all
I'm old.and grey
I no longer care and I'm tired.

Goodnight everyone
I'm going to rest
I'll be gone for quite some time
And although my life has not been the best
I'm content such a life was mine.

Printed in the United Kingdom
by Lightning Source UK Ltd.
9512900001B